The Smart Growth **Tool Kit**

Community Profiles
and Case Studies
to Advance
Smart Growth
Practices

Principal Author
David J. O'Neill

Contributing Authors
Steven Ducham
Oliver Jerschow
Douglas Porter
Laura Cole Reblitz

The Urban Land Institute would like to thank the ULI Foundation, Bank of America, and the Smart Growth Network, whose support made this publication possible.

ULi Foundation

SMART GROWTH
N E T W O R K

**Urban Land
Institute**

About ULI

ULI–the Urban Land Institute is a nonprofit education and research institute that is supported and directed by its members. Its mission is to provide responsible leadership in the use of land in order to enhance the total environment.

ULI sponsors education programs and forums to encourage an open international exchange of ideas and sharing of experiences; initiates research that anticipates emerging land use trends and issues and proposes creative solutions based on that research; provides advisory services; and publishes a wide variety of materials to disseminate information on land use and development. Established in 1936, the Institute today has more than 15,000 members and associates from more than 50 countries representing the entire spectrum of the land use and development disciplines.

ULI Catalog Number: S52

Printed in the United States of America.
International Standard Book Number: 0-87420-842-4

Recommended bibliographic listing:
O'Neill, David. *The Smart Growth Tool Kit.* Washington, D.C.: ULI–the Urban Land Institute, 2000.

ULI Project Staff

Rachelle L. Levitt
Senior Vice President, Policy and Practice
Publisher

Marta V. Goldsmith
Vice President, Land Use Policy

David J. O'Neill
Director, Land Use Policy and Outreach
Project Director

Nancy H. Stewart
Director, Book Program
Managing Editor

Julie D. Stern
Manuscript Editor

Betsy Van Buskirk
Art Director

Meg Batdorff
Graphic Designer

Diann Stanley-Austin
Director of Publishing Operations

ULI Smart Growth Advisory Group

James J. Chaffin, Jr., Chair
President
Chaffin/Light Associates
Spring Island, South Carolina

Maureen McAvey
Director, Business Development
Federal Realty Investment Trust
Rockville, Maryland

Stan Ross
Chairman
University of Southern California Lusk
  Center for Real Estate
Los Angeles, California

Peter S. Rummell
Chairman/CEO
St. Joe Company
Jacksonville, Florida

Charles H. Shaw
Chairman
The Shaw Company
Chicago, Illinois

Smedes York
President
York Properties, Inc.
Raleigh, North Carolina

F. Karl Zavitkovsky
Managing Director
Bank of America
Dallas, Texas

Review Committee

Gary Binger
Director
ULI California Smart Growth Initiative
Oakland, California

Elizabeth B. Davison
Director
Montgomery County Department of
  Housing and Community Affairs
Rockville, Maryland

Robert R. Harris
Managing Partner
Wilkes Artis Chartered
Bethesda, Maryland

Gregg T. Logan
Senior Vice President
Robert Charles Lesser & Company
Atlanta, Georgia

Franklin A. Martin
President
Hidden Springs Community, LLC
Boise, Idaho

Edward T. McMahon
Director, American Greenways
  Program
The Conservation Fund
Arlington, Virginia

Mitchell B. Menzer
Partner
O'Melveny & Myers
Los Angeles, California

Peter Pappas
President and Senior Vice President
Lincoln Harris Corporate Services
Charlotte, North Carolina

James W. Todd
President
The Peterson Companies
Fairfax, Virginia

Daniel C. Van Epp
President
The Howard Hughes Corporation,
  Summerlin Division
Las Vegas, Nevada

CONTENTS

CONTENTS

PART ONE

Preface

In an article that appeared in the *Los Angeles Times* on November 20, 1988, Los Angeles City Council candidate Ryan Snyder explained that he opposes slow growth because it unfairly shifts the development burden from one community to another. Rather, Snyder announced, "I'm for smart growth." That may or may not have been the first time that the term smart growth was used, but since then it has appeared more than 3,000 times in the mainstream press. The extensive exposure has left some feeling overwhelmed by this planning and development term and unsure if it should remain so prominent in the political, development, and planning lexicon. Others still do not understand what smart growth means or even looks like. But now is not the time to ignore the concept. The unintended consequences of growth that smart growth seeks to address—traffic congestion, overcrowded schools, and loss of open space—are not going away. They are and will remain among the most important challenges facing public officials, planning staff, and the development community.

For a number of years, public and private sector leaders have turned to new techniques, under the banner of smart growth, to address these unintended consequences. Others have tried to hide behind the smart growth banner to promote no- or slow-growth agendas. But, practiced in its true form, smart growth offers the means for communities and cities to accommodate inevitable growth in a manner that achieves economic, environmental, and quality-of-life objectives. The communities adopting smart growth approaches vary in size and character, and, as a result, so do the tools that they are using. On the public side, officials are providing leadership; promoting integrated planning and collaboration; offering incentives; removing barriers; participating in public/private partnerships; and targeting public investments. The development community is using its own planning, design, and implementation tools to advance smart growth "on the ground." These include collaborating on planning and design; mixing land uses; developing walkable communities; building near transit and offering other transportation choices; and preserving open space.

This Smart Growth Tool Kit highlights—in five community profiles—more than 20 policies and processes that local governments and regional entities are using to guide future growth, protect natural resources, and encourage economic vitality. Its 19 smart development case studies illustrate the planning, design, and implementation techniques that developers are using to build projects that reflect smart growth characteristics. While each of these community profiles and smart development case studies contains valuable tools, these are not intended as one-size-fits-all solutions. Rather, they demonstrate the broad range of solutions available. Each community, must determine which set of tools is appropriate for it, based on its unique economic, environmental, and social characteristics. And while each profile and case study contains a sampling of tools, these are not intended as an exhaustive listing. Others do exist.

What Is Smart Growth?

At its core, smart growth is about ensuring that neighborhoods, towns, and regions accommodate growth in ways that are economically sound, environmentally responsible, and supportive of community livability—growth that enhances the quality of life. To achieve that objective, many smart growth strategies encourage development in areas with existing or planned infrastructure. Within those areas, they also encourage mixed-use, pedestrian- and transit-oriented development; establish incentives to enhance investment; lower regulatory barriers to development; and use both state and local funding to improve infrastructure.

Not surprisingly, smart growth policies and projects share many characteristics. While each community must consider its smart growth policy in the context of its own unique conditions, and each developer must determine which smart growth tools are appropriate for a specific project, certain common smart growth features

SMART GROWTH FEATURES

⊙ **Collaborating on Solutions**

⊙ **Mixing Land Uses**

⊙ **Encouraging Infill Development and Redevelopment**

⊙ **Building Master-Planned Communities**

⊙ **Conserving Open Space**

⊙ **Providing Transportation Choices**

⊙ **Providing Housing Opportunities**

⊙ **Lowering Barriers to and Providing Incentives for Smart Development**

⊙ **Using High-Quality Design Techniques**

can be extracted from the community profiles and case studies included in the *Tool Kit*. Clearly, not all of the smart growth features described here are applicable to all communities, nor are they presented in order of importance. But all *are* worthy of consideration by public officials, developers, environmentalists, and others who want to shape the development of future smart growth policies and projects.

Collaborating on Solutions

One hallmark of the smart growth movement is collaboration. Collaborative smart growth initiatives seek to identify common ground where the development community, environmentalists, civic organizations, public officials, and citizens can identify the most appropriate ways to accommodate future growth. It is through these collaborative initiatives that policies and practices, such as overcoming opposition to higher-density development, are formulated. Towns, cities, and metropolitan regions throughout the nation have initiated such collaborative processes to achieve multiple community objectives. Smart growth initiatives in the cities of Austin, Charlotte, and Atlanta, all of which are featured here, demonstrate this point. Similarly, developers have learned that collaboration—both with public officials and neighborhood leaders—is important to the success of projects that reflect smart growth features. In fact, most of the smart development case studies highlighted here were the result of collaboration and/or more formal public/private partnerships. And while the specific processes may vary, smart growth collaboration is intended to engender common ground and enable all participants to work to improve land use and development patterns.

Mixing Land Uses

Projects that mix land uses can achieve several smart growth objectives simultaneously. For example, by incorporating a variety of housing types (such as condominiums, townhomes, and single-family houses) and integrating convenience retail facilities (like a corner store, drycleaners, and restaurants), development can attract homeowners of various income levels and reduce their dependence on the automobile, thus providing housing and transportation choices.

Several projects featured in the *Tool Kit,* including Washington's Landing (in Pittsburgh) and Bethesda Row (near Washington, D.C.), are examples of mixed-use development. In addition to mixing a variety of uses into one project, mixed-use development also can integrate public spaces, including parks and environmental preserves. At Washington's Landing, riverfront trails connect the project's open spaces and a public park. The Bethesda Row project incorporates important public spaces that serve as community gathering areas.

Mizner Park, in Boca Raton, Florida, is an example of smart growth. This revitalization project offers housing over shops and provides considerable public space. Mizner Park has become the most popular gathering place in Boca Raton.

Significant impediments to mixed-use development do exist, however. The most obvious and longstanding barrier is local regulations that require single-use zoning. Acquiring financing for mixed-use development also has proven difficult for numerous developers. Nonetheless, mixing land uses is becoming increasingly common throughout the United States, reflecting its growing acceptance and success in the marketplace.

Encouraging Infill Development and Redevelopment

Revitalizing towns, cities, and older suburbs is a central theme in the smart growth movement. Infill and redevelopment strategies offer two ways to achieve that objective. Infill development is defined as the development of new homes, commercial and/or retail buildings, and public facilities on unused or underused lands in existing communities. Redevelopment means restoring existing buildings and properties that are severely blighted and/or diminish the character and function of a neighborhood. This can include adaptive use and historic preservation projects. Brownfields—contaminated former industrial and commercial lands—comprise a portion of the sites that could be redeveloped.

The *Tool Kit* highlights several successful infill and redevelopment projects. The Denver Dry Goods Building and Baltimore's Can Company are examples of redevelopment projects that have served as catalysts to broader urban revitalization. Similarly, Courthouse Hill and the MCI Center (both in the Washington, D.C. metropolitan area) are examples of infill development projects that have added needed housing and entertainment uses, respectively, to their communities. The examples described here demonstrate that infill and redevelopment projects can make efficient use of existing public infrastructure, enhance the tax base, and enliven older neighborhoods.

A number of barriers can make infill development and redevelopment prohibitive. Leading the list are cumbersome and costly local permitting processes, poor infrastructure, and community opposition. Removing these and other barriers will contribute to the revitalization of communities and help make infill development and redevelopment more attractive to the development community.

Building Master-Planned Communities

Usually built on "greenfield" areas adjacent to or near urban fringes, master-planned communities are comprehensively planned and phased in logical stages. According to ULI's *Trends and Innovations in Master-Planned Communities,* they tend to be long-term, multiphased projects that combine a complementary mix of land uses and are held together by unifying design elements. Devel-

The master-planned community of Hidden Springs in Boise, Idaho, offers a mix of housing types, acres of preserved lands, and a town center.

opers are beginning to use master-planning techniques in infill locations. Since many master-planned communities are large-scale development projects, they often can preserve environmental resources, provide biking and pedestrian systems, integrate a mix of housing types, and include shops and employment opportunities (often located in town centers), thereby meeting numerous smart growth objectives. Master-planned communities, like other forms of development, also face growing public opposition. Developers increasingly are confronting NIMBYism (the "not-in-my-backyard" attitude), no matter how well a project is conceived.

The *Tool Kit* includes numerous examples of master-planned communities, including Bonita Bay, Fairview Village, Harbor Town, Orenco Station, Rancho Santa Margarita, Reston Town Center, and Prairie Crossing. These phased and comprehensively planned communities exhibit a wide variety of smart growth characteristics, such as a mix of land use, a pedestrian-oriented design, and an integrated system of public parks and open space.

Conserving Open Space

If recent ballot and legislative initiatives are any indication, public interest in the conservation of open space networks—environmental lands, farmlands, and parks and trails—is growing. In 1998, 72 percent of the 240 state and local open space and conservation ballot measures were approved, pledging nearly $7 billion for the preservation of these lands. The state of New Jersey alone committed $1 billion to establish a system of trails and greenways and to protect significant open space. Other state and local governments also have obligated significant amounts to protect meaningful green space. The *Tool Kit* highlights conservation programs that have been instituted in the city of Austin, Texas; in Montgomery County, Maryland; and in the state of Georgia. In each of these cases, the conservation program is a central element in a larger smart growth initiative.

The Woodlands, near Houston, Texas, is another large-scale master-planned community that reflects many smart growth characteristics, including the conservation of open space. Twenty-five percent of the Woodlands will remain as forest preserves, parks, lakes, and other open spaces.

The value of conserving open space has not been lost on the development community. According to a 1998 American Lives, Inc., survey of homebuyers, natural open space, walking and biking paths, and sidewalks are highly valued community amenities. Incorporating such open space features into development projects has proven to increase the value of new homes, thus achieving both environmental and economic objectives simultaneously. The *Tool Kit* describes how Bonita Bay in Bonita Springs, Florida; Prairie Crossing in Grayslake, Illinois; and Fairview Village in Fairview, Oregon, have integrated open space networks to protect environmental resources, connect residents, and serve as a valued community amenity.

As these examples demonstrate, greenspace preservation is a central component of many smart growth programs. Coupling a community's preservation commitments with incentives to develop in desired locations can help to accommodate growth, while protecting meaningful open space.

Providing Transportation Options

The automobile is, and likely will remain (for the foreseeable future), the number-one transportation choice in the United States. However, frustration with traffic congestion is mounting. In fact, growing traffic congestion may be the number-one issue affecting the public's interest in smart growth policies. "Most of all, suburbanites are tired of traffic—the congestion, the pollution, and the hectic and unfulfilling lifestyle it promotes," notes *Emerging Trends in Real Estate 2000.* The result is a growing interest in other transportation options—light- and heavy-rail systems, expanded bus service, and bike and pedestrian paths—to enhance mobility and improve the quality of life.

Providing transportation options—including light- and heavy-rail systems, expanded bus service, and bicycle and pedestrian paths—is a smart growth technique.

Many smart growth programs support the development of transportation choices and encourage the designation of land uses necessary to support them. Charlotte, North Carolina, for instance, has approved a dedicated transit fund (highlighted in the *Tool Kit*) to support the development of light-rail and bus rapid transit in the Charlotte-Mecklenburg region. As part of this effort, public officials, planners, business leaders, and ULI–the Urban Land Institute are working together to determine the most appropriate land use patterns to support the region's transit investment. These land use designations may include providing for compact, mixed-use development along transportation corridors and near transit stations.

Providing Housing Opportunities

Providing housing opportunities to people in a range of income levels throughout a region is another objective of smart growth. Despite historic highs in homeownership and a strong economy, affordable housing for moderate- and lower-income citizens is scarce in certain parts of the country. According to the U.S. Department of Housing and Urban Development (HUD), approximately 5.4 million very low-income families pay more than half their income for housing. But the lack of affordable housing choices is not limited to the very poor. In several major metropolitan areas, particularly those in expanding high-tech markets, housing for middle-income wage earners also is in very short supply. In the Silicon Valley region, for example, modest homes may cost between $400,000 and $500,000. The most affordable housing options for middle-income workers in Silicon Valley are located far from employment centers. As a result, workers commonly spend hours commuting. While this may be an extreme case, affordable housing issues are on the rise in numerous cities across the country.

The lack of housing opportunities contributes to the jobs/housing imbalance that faces many major metropolitan regions. This imbalance can be attributed to several forces, including community opposition to higher-density development, a desire to attract jobs over housing, local regulations, and tax policies. The *Tool Kit* highlights two programs, the Housing Action Coalition in Silicon Valley and Montgomery County's highly regarded inclusionary housing requirement, to demonstrate how some communities are dealing with the affordability issue. From the development perspective, two *Tool Kit* case studies—Pearl Court Apartments in Portland, Oregon, and Addison Circle, near Dallas—show that mixed-income housing can be both attractive and profitable.

Lowering Barriers to and Providing Incentives for Smart Development

Providing financial incentives and streamlining procedures to improve predictability in the development process is a key principle of smart growth. Smart growth differs from traditional growth management programs in that it combines incentives, disincentives, and traditional planning techniques to promote a pattern of growth that achieves economic, environmental, and quality-of-life objectives. Maryland's smart growth program, for example, uses state financial assistance to encourage growth in designated "priority funding areas." While growth is permitted outside these areas, state infrastructure funding is not available to support such development. Maryland's program was further advanced by the recent passage of its smart codes initiative. Among other things, this initiative establishes a streamlined rehabilitation code that will reduce the time and cost of rehabilitating old structures. Austin, Texas, uses a range of incentives, including infrastructure enhancements, streamlined or "green-tape" permitting, and fee waivers, to encourage development in designated "smart growth zones." Incentive-based policies are at the heart of the smart growth movement, as demonstrated by a number of smart growth policies being adopted by state and local governments across the country.

Using High-Quality Design Techniques

High-quality design is a central component of smart growth, as the *Tool Kit*'s case studies demonstrate. Using high-quality design techniques can help alleviate public opposition to new growth and development, including adversarial attitudes toward higher-density development. By using design techniques such as integrating land uses, mixing housing types, protecting open spaces, and creating a pedestrian-oriented environment, designers and developers can build new places that are supported, rather than opposed, by neighborhood leaders and local jurisdictions.

High-quality design takes various forms. Traditional neighborhood or new urbanist design, which espouses development with a consistent design character; a mix of land uses, housing types, and lot sizes; narrower streets; and a system of public spaces, is growing in popularity. Projects such as Harbor Town in Memphis and Fairview Village near Portland offer examples of how traditional neighborhood design can help create a sense of community. Conservation design, which concentrates development on one portion of a site, while leaving the remaining area as protected open space, is another design technique that developers are using and local governments are promoting to support smart growth principles. East Lake Commons in Atlanta and Prairie Crossing near Chicago are examples of developments that have used this technique successfully. Regardless of the specific design approach, high-quality design—design that mixes land uses, encourages pedestrian activity, protects public and open spaces, and creates a sense of community—is a characteristic common to smart development projects.

What Is the Purpose of the *Tool Kit*?

As noted earlier, public officials, builders, civic organizations, and environmentalists all are demonstrating broad support for smart growth. As a result (in part) of this diverse support, smart growth has generated numerous and sometimes contradictory viewpoints. In certain cases, particularly at the local level, the smart growth argument has been used to advance a slow-growth or no-growth agenda. This misuse of the term could undermine a movement that has successfully brought divergent interests together to address challenging growth issues. For the most part, however, the term has represented a willingness of diverse interests to work collaboratively to set a course for responsibly accommodating future growth and development.

The goal of the *Smart Growth Tool Kit* is to inform the public, private, and nonprofit sectors about the tools that are available to advance collaborative smart growth initiatives. This publication brings together community profiles that highlight smart growth public policies and processes, plus case studies of development projects that reflect smart growth characteristics. Through these examples, and a resource guide, the *Smart Growth Tool Kit* will help to better define what smart growth is and is not, communicate how it is being implemented, and share tools that can help to start or advance a community smart growth initiative.

The *Tool Kit* is an outgrowth of the work that ULI–the Urban Land Institute has undertaken to provide objective information and best practices on the subject. It draws on the experiences of ULI members and staff who have participated in national forums, regional symposiums, community outreach events, and local growth and development processes. ULI plans to update the *Tool Kit* periodically, to keep it abreast of the latest tools and techniques, policies and development practices, that are working to advance smart growth nationally and at the local level.

What Information Is in the *Tool Kit*?

The *Tool Kit* is comprised of four parts: this "Preface," "Smart Growth Community Profiles," "Smart Development Case Studies," and the "Resource Guide." Each section is designed to inform the reader about public policy and development practices that are being used to advance smart growth.

The profiles of five communities—Atlanta, Georgia; Austin, Texas; Charlotte, North Carolina; Montgomery County, Maryland; and Silicon Valley, California—in the second part offer a sampling of the tools that communities are using to address specific growth-related challenges. Each profile includes a community description, demographic and market trend information, an overview of the community's smart growth strategy, a brief description of the smart growth tools it is using, and one or more information contacts. These communities were not selected because they are considered the "poster children of smart growth." Instead, they were chosen because they demonstrate the range of challenges associated with rapid growth, and some of the tools being used to address those challenges.

As mentioned earlier, while each of these profiles presents a valuable model, they are not intended as one-size-fits-all solutions. Rather, they demonstrate the range of solutions that exists. The appropriate set of tools for any one community must be determined on the basis of its unique economic, environmental, and social characteristics.

The third part of the *Tool Kit*—the case studies—is organized into four categories: infill development; brownfield redevelopment; inner-ring development; and suburban development. Each case study includes a brief description of the project, the characteristics that make it an example of smart growth, the barriers that the developer(s) had to overcome to build the project, lessons learned, project data, and an information contact.

The *Tool Kit*'s fourth and final section is a resource guide that contains a number of tools that will be helpful in developing a smart growth program, including a model step-by-step program to help a community initiate a smart growth effort. These steps are generic in nature, but reflect some of the lessons learned from communities implementing smart growth programs and from the experiences of ULI and its District Councils. The resource guide also includes sample meeting agendas, tips on working with the media, descriptions of smart growth programs, a list of smart growth resource contacts, and a ULI resources page.

How Is the *Tool Kit* Used?

The *Tool Kit* can be used as a "how-to" workbook, as a reference book, and/or as a public education tool. Overall, ULI hopes that this publication will inform practitioners of the tools and development techniques that currently are advancing smart growth practices across the nation. From a public perspective, the *Tool Kit* can be used to identify specific policies with which governments are defining and implementing smart growth programs. Developers may find that the smart development case studies can help them to understand what features make up a smart growth project, to avoid some of the pitfalls of this type of development, and to gain a general understanding of how these projects were built.

ULI also hopes that the *Tool Kit* will be used to aid ULI District Council–led smart growth initiatives. Overall, the *Tool Kit* is designed to help public leaders, private sector practitioners, the environmental and civic communities, and the general public to understand the policies and development practices that are working to improve the quality of life of our communities.

Sources

The Affordable Community (Washington, D.C.: ULI–the Urban Land Institute, 1981).

Michael Bernick and Robert Cervero, *Transit Villages in the 21st Century* (New York: McGraw-Hill, 1996).

Emerging Trends in Real Estate 2000 (New York: Lend Lease Real Estate Investments and PricewaterhouseCoopers, October 1999).

Joel S. Hirschhorn, *Growing Pains: Quality of Life in the New Economy (Washington, D.C.: National Governor's Association, 2000).*

Moving Beyond Sprawl: The Challenge for Metropolitan Atlanta (Washington, D.C.: The Brookings Institute Center on Urban and Metropolitan Policy, 2000).

Silicon Valley Projections '99 (San Jose: Silicon Valley Manufacturing Group and the Association of Bay Area Governments, 1999).

The State of the Cities 2000: Megaforces Shaping the Future of the Nation's Cities (Washington, D.C.: U.S. Department of Housing and Urban Development, 2000).

The State of the Nation's Housing: 2000 (Cambridge, Massachusetts: Joint Center for Housing Studies, Harvard University, June 2000); available at www.gsd.harvard.edu/jcenter/.

Texas Transportation Institute, *1999 Annual Mobility Report* (College Station, Texas: Texas Transportation Institute, November 1999); available at www.mobility.tamu.edu.

Trends and Innovations in Master-Planned Communities (Washington, D.C.: ULI–the Urban Land Institute, 1998).

PART TWO

Community Profiles

Each community profile describes four or five tools used by the community to promote smart growth, each of which can be categorized under one or more of three broad headings—providing leadership; promoting planning and encouraging collaboration; and providing incentives, removing barriers, and targeting public investments. The communities are using these tools to mitigate traffic congestion, enhance the efficient use of infrastructure, protect open space, provide affordable housing, revitalize neighborhoods, and improve the decision-making process. The general headings provide a context under which the specific tools are applied.

Provide Leadership

As a general rule, the foundation for any successful smart growth initiative is the commitment made by key leaders. Leadership on these growth issues can come in many forms—both traditional (state and local governments) and nontraditional (the business community and civic organizations). In some cases, such as the state of Georgia's smart growth effort (see Atlanta, Georgia, page 13), both the public and private sectors have played key roles in defining a smart growth program and in working together to implement it. This collaborative leadership approach is a hallmark of the smart growth movement and an essential tool in establishing any smart growth initiative.

Promote Integrated Planning and Encourage Collaboration

Extensive, collaborative, and integrated planning—at the state, regional, community, and neighborhood levels—is often the framework within which a comprehensive smart growth strategy is developed. At the regional level, for example, citizens, developers, and public officials have developed smart growth alternative scenarios that allow them to set a course for the future pattern, location, and form of development. In the Greater Salt Lake City region, Envision Utah, a public/private partnership, led a bottom-up process designed to gather citizen input and develop alternative growth scenarios that illustrate potential development patterns over the next 20 years. Envision Utah is conducting a community outreach process to encourage residents to express their preferences on how they want their community and region to grow. While planning is traditionally a function of regional and local governments, smart growth seeks to improve the planning process by encouraging a collaborative planning effort that integrates historically isolated planning disciplines, such as land use and transportation (see Charlotte, North Carolina, page 26).

Provide Incentives, Remove Barriers, and Target Public Investments

Some of the most recognizable state- and local-led smart growth programs use incentives, remove barriers to smart growth development, and target public investments to implement their smart growth programs. The city of Austin, Texas (see page 20), uses incentives such as waived fees, expedited construction permits, and electric utility incentives to encourage development in its dedicated smart growth zones. The state of New Jersey has removed barriers to redevelopment by adopting a new rehabilitation building code that has reduced the cost of revitalizing older structures and spurred development of older urban areas. (Delaware and Maryland recently adopted similar codes.) The state of Maryland's Smart Growth Program targets public investments, such as state infrastructure, economic development, and other investments, to encourage development in "priority funding areas," defined by local jurisdictions, where infrastructure is available or planned.

Community Profile Challenges and Tools Matrix

Community/Tools	Mitigate Traffic Congestion	Enhance the Efficient Use of Infrastructure	Protect Open Space	Provide Affordable Housing	Revitalize Neighborhoods	Improve the Decision-Making Process
Atlanta, Georgia						
Georgia Regional Transportation Authority	●	●			●	●
Community greenspace initiative			●			
Financial incentive strategies	●	●			●	
Coalition building						●
Austin, Texas						
Land Development Simplification Process		●			●	●
Smart growth zones		●	●	●	●	
Land conservation program		●	●			
Neighborhood planning	●				●	●
Smart growth matrix and incentives	●	●				●
Charlotte, North Carolina						
Dedicated transit fund	●	●				
2025 Land Use/ Transit Plan	●	●	●			
Smart growth audit		●				●
Inclusive decision-making process						●
Montgomery County, Maryland						
Transportation-supported development	●	●	●		●	
Community livability programs	●	●			●	●
Inclusionary housing requirements	●	●		●		
Open space conservation measures		●	●			
Inclusive decision-making process						●
Silicon Valley, California						
Transit-oriented development corridors	●	●	●			
Urban growth boundaries		●	●		●	
Housing Action Coalition				●		●
Land supply inventory		●			●	

PROFILE: Atlanta, Georgia
Collaboration Addresses Regional Concerns

Smart Growth Tools

⊙ Georgia Regional Transportation Authority

⊙ Community greenspace initiative

⊙ Financial incentives

⊙ Coalition building

The Community

The 3,000-square-mile Atlanta region comprises ten counties and 64 municipalities, including the city of Atlanta. (The region should not be confused with the 18-county Atlanta metropolitan statistical area.)

Even before the Civil War, the Atlanta region was the transportation hub of the southeastern United States. During the late 1800s, natural resources and manufactured goods traveled to and from Atlanta on rail lines that converged on the city from points north, south, east, and west. Today, transportation continues to play a central role in the economic health of the region. The region's airport—Hartsfield International—is the busiest in the world; its highway system is extensive, though increasingly congested; and it remains a rail hub. This expansive transportation network, relatively low business costs, and appealing suburban communities have attracted major corporations, such as CNN and Coca-Cola, to establish international headquarters in the region.

Atlanta's hosting of the 1996 Summer Olympic Games signified the region's arrival on the world stage. Now clearly established in the international arena, the Atlanta region has continued its evolutionary path from its modest beginnings to a bustling economic activity center that is home to more than 3.2 million people.

Atlanta's population has grown by 25 percent since 1990 and is expected to reach 5 million by 2020.

Smart Growth Strategy

The number-one issue facing the future health and prosperity of the Atlanta region, according to a spring 2000 *Atlanta Journal-Constitution* poll, is traffic congestion. Citizens of Atlanta drive more miles per day and pollute more per capita than do residents of most U.S. metropolitan areas. Atlanta's air quality can be very poor (particularly during the summer), water quality and quantity concerns are on the rise as development within the Chattahoochee River basin increases exponentially, and the region's quality of life—which attracted many corporations and a strong labor force—is showing signs of erosion. In 1998, the Hewlett-Packard Company, citing traffic congestion issues, reconsidered further expansion in the Perimeter Center—the region's largest employment center and shopping destination. The U.S. Environmental Protection Agency (EPA) has classified the region as a serious nonattainment area for ozone, further contributing to concerns that its quality of life is threatened. The region has failed to prepare a plan that adequately addresses these air quality concerns, and thus has been denied $600 million in federal funding for transportation assistance.

The Hewlett-Packard decision, the status levied on the region by the EPA, and public concerns over traffic congestion and air and water quality have served as a wake-up call to leaders in Atlanta's business, public, and civic sectors. Responding to these concerns, diverse organizations—including the Atlanta Regional Commission (ARC), the newly formed Georgia Regional Transportation Authority (GRTA), Georgia Institute of Technology (Georgia Tech), the Atlanta Metropolitan Chamber of Commerce, the Georgia Conservancy, the ULI Atlanta District Council, and many others—are forming collaborative partnerships to address the multijurisdictional and multifaceted challenges associated with rapid economic expansion.

Leading the way in these efforts is the Metro Atlanta Chamber of Commerce. Recognizing that the EPA threat to retain federal transportation funds—as well as the growing number of damaging media reports about Atlanta's sprawl and air quality issues—might harm the region's economic future, in June 1998 the chamber formed the Metro Atlanta Transportation Initiative to establish recommendations for a transportation plan capable of meeting Clean Air Act requirements. The 33-member group was composed of business, academic, civic, and public sector leaders. In November 1999, the Metro Atlanta Transportation Initiative issued a report calling on the state to "create a regional transportation authority" or another

---

THE ATLANTA REGION: FACTS AND FIGURES

⊙ Since 1990, the region's job base has grown by more than 23 percent, from 1.41 to 1.84 million jobs. More than 115,000 new jobs were created in 1999 alone.

⊙ The region's population has grown by 25 percent since 1990. It is projected to reach 5 million by 2020, an increase of more than 1.5 million people.

⊙ More than 60,000 housing permits were issued in 1999, the most of any U.S. metropolitan region.

⊙ From 1990 to 1997, the region grew from 65 to 110 miles across.

⊙ Nearly 50 acres of open space is converted to developed land every day.

⊙ The Atlanta metropolitan statistical area (MSA) ranks sixth in the country in traffic congestion.

mechanism that has the responsibility for planning, resource allocation, and monitoring implementation for all forms of transportation.

During the 1999 Georgia General Assembly session, Governor Roy Barnes and the legislature created the Georgia Regional Transportation Authority (GRTA). The mission of GRTA is "to provide the citizens of Georgia with transportation choices, improved air quality, and better land use in order to enhance their quality of life and promote growth that can be sustained by future generations." It has many of the broad powers that the Metro Atlanta Chamber of Commerce recommended. For instance, GRTA has the authority to veto major highways and major "developments of regional impact," to create and operate mass transit, and to deny state funds to local governments that are unwilling to cooperate with its policies. While its power is limited to the 13-county area that EPA identified as a serious nonattainment region, if that nonattainment area grows or captures other parts of the state, so will GRTA's purview.

While GRTA has broad powers, it realizes that long-term success will require the commitment and cooperation of a great number of local governments, civic and environmental organizations, institutions, and individuals. Since these groups all have a stake in seeing smart growth succeed, many of them are supporting GRTA. One such supporter is Smart Growth Partners, an organization comprised of the ULI Atlanta District Council, the Metro Atlanta Chamber of Commerce, the Georgia Conservancy, and Georgia Tech. Since mid-1999, Smart Growth Partners has sponsored outreach initiatives intended to educate various sectors of the community, including developers and public officials, about the issues surrounding smart growth. "Smart Growth Partners is complementing GRTA's work by creating the civic infrastructure necessary for smart growth solutions to be implemented in local communities," explains Gregg Logan, chair of the ULI Atlanta District Council and managing director of Robert Charles Lesser & Company.

More than 20 other organizations and governmental agencies in the Atlanta region are developing tools, providing incentives, and funding programs to build a future of profitable development, livable communities, and environmental integrity.

Centennial Park was at the center of the 1996 Olympic Games, which signified Atlanta's arrival in the international arena.

Smart Growth Tools

Georgia Regional Transportation Authority

The Georgia General Assembly created GRTA in 1999, at the urging of Governor Barnes, to help the Atlanta region address air quality, traffic congestion, and quality-of-life issues. GRTA will use both incentives and regulations to implement its mission. The 15-member GRTA board has the authority, for instance, to issue $1 billion in revenue bonds and, with the consent of the general assembly, $1 billion in general obligation bonds to assist local governments in financing mass transit or other related projects that will alleviate air quality problems. These financial incentives are coupled with a set of regulatory authorities that GRTA has at its disposal, the greatest of which is GRTA's authority to approve or disqualify all major transportation and development projects proposed in the 13-county Atlanta metropolitan region. Reversing a GRTA transportation- or development-related decision requires local governments to produce a three-fourths "supermajority."

GRTA's board has formed several policy councils and technical advisory working groups to assist it in setting policies and standards, and in ensuring that its decisions reflect the needs of a cross section of community stakeholders. "Today, quality of life is central to ensuring future economic prosperity," explains Joel Cowen, GRTA chairman. "That is why we need to address issues such as traffic congestion, air quality, and a good environment for our children."

A central component of GRTA's work will focus on the implementation of a three-year regional transportation plan that seeks to achieve compliance with Clean Air Act requirements. By successfully implementing the plan, the Atlanta region again will be eligible for the broad use of federal transportation funds. While its efforts have just begun, GRTA has been given the tools and can offer the incentives necessary to achieve its broad objectives.

SMART GROWTH PLAYERS

⊙ **Atlanta Regional Commission (ARC).** As the regional planning agency for the ten-county, 64-municipality region, ARC compiles the most current regional data, forecasts future trends, and tracks critical issues facing the area, including water and air quality issues.

⊙ **Smart Growth Partners.** The mission of this partnership—comprised of the ULI Atlanta District Council, Georgia Tech, the Metro Atlanta Chamber of Commerce, and the Georgia Conservancy—is to research and promote land use, development, and transportation policies, practices, and investments that support smart growth in the region.

⊙ **Strategies for Metro Atlanta's Regional Transportation and Air Quality (SMARTRAQ).** Led by Georgia Tech's College of Architecture and School of Civil and Environmental Engineering, SMARTRAQ is conducting research to integrate land use with transportation, air quality, and household activity. The work of SMARTRAQ is being closely coordinated with the efforts of the Smart Growth Partners.

⊙ **The Georgia Quality Growth Partnership (GQGP).** Various organizations' desire to coordinate their efforts to promote smart growth approaches in the Atlanta region spurred the formation of the GQGP, which is composed of more than 30 organizations representing environmental, civic, academic, and government interests. The group is developing a smart growth tool kit, providing a forum for the exchange of ideas and best practices, and helping to reduce duplication of efforts.

Community Greenspace Initiative

During the 2000 Georgia General Assembly session, Governor Barnes took added steps to achieve his smart growth objectives by promoting the passage of legislation encouraging Georgia's 40 fastest-growing counties to set aside 20 percent of their land as permanent greenspace. Counties in the Atlanta region with a population of more than 60,000 and/or an average growth rate of 800 persons/per year are eligible to participate in this program. The legislation authorized $30 million for land acquisition during the program's first year. Based on this first-year commitment, 11 counties in the Atlanta region could be eligible for approximately $20 million to buy undeveloped land for parks, environmental protection, and hiking and biking trails.

While the legislation contains no requirement to fund the program annually, Governor Barnes has pledged to request at least $30 million every year hereafter. Counties and municipalities that are interested in participating must establish a Community Greenspace Trust Fund and develop a greenspace program that announces its commitment to permanently protect at least 20 percent of its greenspace and identifies those parcels of land it intends to protect. By establishing a Greenspace Trust Fund in each participating county, public officials hope to leverage the state's commitment with foundation and private sector contributions to meet statewide greenspace protection objectives.

Financial Incentives

Incentives are central to the implementation of Atlanta's smart growth efforts. Both GRTA and the governor's greenspace program offer incentives to local governments to implement smart growth activities such as balancing transportation investments with land use decisions and preserving environmentally sensitive lands. Efforts initiated by ARC also provide incentives for smart growth planning and development in town centers. Through its Livable Center Initiative, ARC has established an incentive-based program to encourage local governments and nonprofit organizations to increase mixed-use development and promote connectivity in town and activity centers. ARC incentives include $5 million dedicated to funding studies over the next five years to determine ways to encourage town center development and redevelopment. Communities participating in the Activity Center/Town Center Investment Policy Studies program are eligible for significant-

GRTA'S POWERS AND RESPONSIBILITIES

⊙ **Plan, design, construct, lease, operate, manage, and maintain public transportation systems and air quality control installations through contracts with public and private entities.**

⊙ **Coordinate planning for transportation and air quality purposes among all state, regional, and local authorities.**

⊙ **Review regional plans prepared by the ARC and the state transportation department, negotiate revisions, and approve the plans by a two-thirds majority vote.**

⊙ **Review and approve developments of regional impact as a prerequisite for the expenditure of state transportation funds.**

⊙ **Set targets for air quality improvements and standards.**

⊙ **Make grants or loans to local governments.**

⊙ **Acquire property through eminent domain.**

Riverside by Post is a smart growth project located along the banks of the Chattahoochee River in northwest Atlanta. The pedestrian-oriented project features a traditional neighborhood design with tree-lined streets and ground-floor retail space with apartments above.

ly more funding to implement strategies. ARC, in fact, has approved $350 million over the next five years for implementation activities in town centers.

Incentives offered through ARC and GRTA are two examples of how decision makers are using the "carrot" of financial incentives (rather than the "stick" of restrictive regulations) to encourage patterns and forms of development that reflect smart growth characteristics.

Coalition Building

A unique element of Atlanta's smart growth process is the efforts being made to form coalitions composed of organizations that historically have held divergent viewpoints on growth and development issues. Smart Growth Partners, for instance, is one example of how environmentalists, business leaders, developers, and academics are joining forces to help address the multifaceted issues associated with implementing a smart growth strategy. Many of these collaborative undertakings aim to educate citizens, developers, and public officials on the challenges the region faces with respect to transportation, development, and environmental health, and about the tools and techniques that can be applied to overcome those challenges. Coalition building seems to be working, as various interest groups are agreeing on the fundamental challenges and some of the solutions that are necessary to advance smart growth in the region.

In the Atlanta region, coalition building is helping to raise the public's awareness that policies and practices must change to ensure that the region's quality of life and economic prosperity are maintained and enhanced.

Information Contacts

Charles Walston
Communications Director
Georgia Regional Transportation Authority
245 Peachtree Center Avenue
Suite 900
Atlanta, Georgia 30303
404-463-3000

Gregg Logan
Managing Director, Robert Charles Lesser & Company
3384 Peachtree Road NE, Suite 500
Atlanta, Georgia 30326
404-365-9501

Resources

Web Sites

Georgia Regional Transportation Authority **www.grta.org**
Atlanta Regional Commission **www.atlanta-info.com**
Metro Atlanta Chamber of Commerce **www.metroatlantachamber.com**
Georgia Conservancy **www.gaconservancy.org**
Georgia Institute of Technology **www.gatech.edu**

Sources

"Atlanta Metropolitan Area," *ULI Market Profiles 1999: North America* (Washington, D.C.: ULI–the Urban Land Institute, 1999).

Leon Eplan, "Atlanta Airs Its Options," *Planning,* November 1999.

David Firestone, "Suburban Comforts Thwart Atlanta's Plans to Limit Sprawl," *New York Times,* November 20, 1999.

Joel S. Hirschhorn, *Growing Pains: Quality of Life in the New Economy* (Washington, D.C.: National Governors' Association, 2000).

"Horizon Metro Poll," *Atlanta Journal-Constitution,* March 2000.

Gregg Logan, "Atlanta at the Crossroads," *Urban Land,* April 1999.

Moving Beyond Sprawl: The Challenge for Metropolitan Atlanta (Washington, D.C.: The Brookings Institute Center on Urban and Metropolitan Policy, 2000).

Regional Data: Regional Data Sheet 1999 (Atlanta: Atlanta Regional Commission, 1999).

SB 399–Georgia Greenspace Program: Expanded Summary. May 12, 2000.

Texas Transportation Institute, *1999 Annual Urban Mobility Report* (Washington, D.C.: U.S. Census Bureau, 1999).

Smart Growth Zones Direct Growth, Spur Revitalization

Smart Growth Tools

⊙ Land Development Simplification Project

⊙ Smart growth zones

⊙ Land conservation program

⊙ Neighborhood planning

⊙ Smart growth matrix and incentives

The Community

Located in the central Texas Hill Country, along the Colorado River, Austin is Texas's state capital and its fourth-largest city. Prior to the 1970s, Austin's economy was based primarily on higher education (it is home to the University of Texas), state government, and tourism. More recently, however, the city has gained recognition as a global high-tech center by attracting companies such as Dell Computer Corporation, Motorola, IBM, Intel, and Texas Instruments. Austin's ascent as a high-tech magnet has spurred phenomenal population and job growth.

Smart Growth Strategy

In February 1998, the Austin City Council launched a smart growth initiative to direct development in ways that would preserve the city's livability and natural resources while providing for economic opportunity. This initiative was developed by a subcommittee of the city council in conjunction with a larger focus group drawn from the Austin community. The concepts found in the smart growth initiative were first described by the Citizen's Planning Committee (CPC), which began its work in late 1994.

Today, Austin is viewed as a leader in making the smart growth concept a reality. The city has developed strategic programs that define where growth should occur—areas called smart growth zones—to preserve and enhance neighborhoods, strengthen the city's economy and tax base, and protect its natural environment. Through the efficient use of public funds, generous incentive packages, and the formation of regional partnerships, the city has attracted jobs, housing, and retail to smart growth zones. Furthermore, the city has made tremendous strides in streamlining its development process, implementing a neighborhood-based planning framework, and outlining a plan for the purchase of water conservation easements in Austin's most environmentally sensitive areas.

The combination of innovative policies and a strong economy has helped one of the most interesting smart growth strategies in the country to demonstrate a number of visible successes. "In Austin, a happy coincidence of political, social, and economic demands is leading high-tech companies to seek downtown locations. Austin's 'digital downtown,' as it is becoming known, is a good example of how sound smart growth policies can play a role in directing and facilitating growth in urban areas," explains Jim Smith, Austin's assistant city manager.

Numerous roadblocks lie ahead in the implementation of the city's smart growth strategy. The primary challenge involves establishing greater trust and consensus among the many groups involved in the city's growth and development, which include neighborhood associations; builders, developers, and other real estate professionals; public officials; environmentalists; and concerned citizens, to name just a few. But there seems to be more than enough momentum and a strong leadership base to overcome such challenges. "My goal for downtown has been to create 3,000 housing units, enhance our tax base, and turn around the sense of stagnation that people were feeling about the central city," explains Mayor Kirk Watson, who has helped spearhead the city's smart growth initiative since his election in 1997.

Smart Growth Tools

Land Development Simplification Project

Austin already is beginning to reap the benefits of its smart growth policies. In May 1998, Mayor Watson and Council Members Jack Goodman and Daryl Slusher began meeting with a 21-member focus group to overhaul the city's land development code. Over a period of seven months, the Land Development Simplification Project created the foundation for Austin's smart growth policies by establishing general planning principles; providing incentives and a viable mechanism for infill development; developing a neighborhood-based planning framework; analyzing the provision, management, and regulation of wastewater service; outlining a plan for the purchase of water conservation easements in environmentally sensitive areas; creating a simpler version of the land development code; and streamlining the development approval process.

The results of this process have encouraged the siting of two new California-based high-tech companies in the city's downtown Desired Development Zone—Computer Sciences Corporation (CSC), a software and computer services company, and Intel, a global leader in the manufacturing of computer chips. CSC is constructing a 350,000-square-foot office building that will become its division headquarters and Intel is planning a $100 million, 400,000-square-foot computer chip design center. The companies selected the downtown location over suburban sites for a number of reasons, not least of which was the targeted incentive package offered by the city. This incentive package included waived fees, expedited construction permits, and electric utility incentives.

Smart Growth Zones

In an effort to decrease suburban sprawl and encourage investment in existing developed areas, the Austin City Council has adopted two "smart growth zones"—the Drinking Water Protection Zone and the Desired Development Zone—to provide the city with clear policy direction about where future development is to be encouraged or restricted. The zones are located within the city's entire extraterritorial jurisdiction, an area extending in a five-mile radius from the city's incorporated boundary. They also include areas forming a greenbelt of parks and preserves throughout the region. Generally, the two zones are defined as follows:

The Drinking Water Protection Zone includes sensitive environmental areas, endangered species habitat, and the Edward Aquifer Recharge zone.

The Desired Development Zone includes the traditional urban core and commercial districts, as well as the central business district. Within this zone, the city has defined four subzones, in which various levels of incentives may become available to development projects that meet smart growth design and location requirements. These are the *Urban Core* (defined by the boundary of the urban watersheds), in which the city will encourage residential infill and redevelopment activities; *Downtown and the Central Business District* (including the city's central business district, the central urban redevelopment enterprise areas, the state governmental complex, and the University of Texas campus), where the city will encourage the development of commercial, retail, and office space, housing, and parking; *Smart Growth Corridors* (defined by the existing commercial routes that

Austin's smart growth zones.

connect transit nodes), along which the city will encourage mixed-use development; and *Transit Nodes* (areas within a one-quarter-mile radius of light-rail stations), where the city will encourage high-density, transit-oriented development.

"We offer financial support, in the form of infrastructure enhancements, streamlined permitting, fee waivers, and parking requirement modifications to those developers who are willing to develop in the Desired Development Zone and provide things like transit tie-ins, mixed-income housing, pedestrian zones, design standards, and neighborhood group buy-in," says Mayor Watson. Two significant residential projects that flank the high-tech commercial development in the downtown subzone are underway. Just two blocks from the Intel building, Atlanta-based Post Properties is in the final stage of developing 239 apartments, while Chicago-based AMLI Residential Properties Trust and Austin-based Bonner Carrington Corporation are codeveloping a mixed-use residential and retail development adjacent to CSC's divisional headquarters. Both of these projects are using incentives that are part of the city's smart growth and downtown revitalization initiatives.

While these projects demonstrate some early successes of the smart growth initiative, the range of incentives and mechanisms for encouraging development in the Desired Development Zone are still being crafted. The general objective is for the city and its residents to complete neighborhood plans that, at a minimum, cover areas within a one-quarter-mile radius of transit stations and within 300 feet of the pavement along designated corridors. A significant number of incentives then will be available to developers who submit proposals that reflect the neighborhood plan's requirements and that include specific design elements. Incentive packages for development projects along transit corridors and in transit nodes will be designed to create more pedestrian-, transit-, and bicycle-friendly conditions.

Land Conservation Program

As part of its smart growth efforts, the city, in partnership with citizen organizations, aims to conserve lands of significant environmental, cultural, and recreational value. During the 1990s, voters approved more than $130 million to fund conservation easements and outright purchases of properties that protect the city's drinking water supply, preserve its natural heritage, and maintain its quality of life. In July 1999, for example, the city acquired 920 acres of land in southwest Travis County that was targeted for intensive development and turned it into a watershed buffer that provides protection for the Barton Springs watershed. This

tract of land rated highest in the city's evaluation matrix of conservation properties most desirable for purchase. With this acquisition, Austin has achieved approximately 90 percent of its goal to acquire 15,000 acres of sensitive lands.

While some of the land conservation money is being used to purchase land in Austin's Drinking Water Protection Zone, other funds are being used to protect the most important lands in the Desired Development Zone. By committing resources to protect important green infrastructure—parks and stream corridors—in areas targeted for development, the city seeks to provide natural amenities that will attract developers to invest in desired locations.

Neighborhood Planning

Neighborhood planning has become the cornerstone of Austin's smart growth initiative. The neighborhood planning process empowers each neighborhood to develop a specific plan to address issues of concern to the community. The city provides overall guidance to assure that citywide goals are met. Citizens, local stakeholders, city departments, community organizations, and local institutions all work together to address land use planning and service delivery issues. The goal of neighborhood planning is to promote mutual responsibility and joint problem solving.

To date, the city council has initiated a neighborhood planning program in three neighborhoods. Pilot plans have been prepared for the Dawson neighborhood in south Austin and the East Cesar Chavez and Chestnut neighborhoods in east Austin. Generally, these plans include provisions to:

⊙ Enhance the community's livability;

⊙ Create amenities for residents;

⊙ Protect the character of the neighborhood;

⊙ Plan for neighborhood traffic management;

⊙ Furnish limited opportunities for compact, mixed-use development along smart growth corridors and at transit nodes; and

⊙ Encourage infill development where appropriate.

Smart Growth Matrix and Incentives

The smart growth matrix is a tool to assist the city council in analyzing development proposals within the Desired Development Zone. It is designed to provide a quantitative measure of the council's goals and policy directions as they might apply to individual projects. The matrix contains a list of urban design elements, location-specific criteria, and policy components organized within the structure of the council's three goals for smart growth: to determine how and where development should occur, to improve the quality of life, and to enhance the tax base. A weighting system determines the relative rank of each category of items and its value. If a proposed development project, as measured by the matrix, significantly advances the city's goals, financial incentives may be available to help offset the high cost of developing in urban areas. These incentives, which require city council review and approval, may include reduced development fees and public investment in new or improved infrastructure (such as water and sewer lines, streets or streetscape improvements, or similar facilities).

A city staff panel consisting of the project manager and at least three other key staff members representing the departments of planning, public works, and utility services determines the points a project should receive, based on information submitted by the applicant (the developer), additional material supplied by the applicant, and interviews with the applicant. The panel can give a project all of the available points (if it meets or exceeds the defined criteria), one-half or one-third of the available points (if it partially meets the criteria), or no points (if it does not meet the criteria). For more details, see "Austin, Texas's Smart Growth Matrix" on page 136. Austin's smart growth matrix can be viewed on the city's Web site.

Information Contacts

George Adams
Principal Planner
Planning, Environmental and
    Conservation Services Department
City of Austin
Austin, Texas 78701
512-499-2146

Philip W. Capron
President, Synemark
5929 Balcones Drive, Suite 100
Austin, Texas 78731
512-451-5555
Fax: 512-451-3773

Resources

Web Sites
Austin's Smart Growth Initiative   **www.ci.austin.tx.us/smartgrowth.htm**
The Trust for Public Land's Greenprint   **www.igc.org/tpl/greenprint/index/html**
    Resources, Greenprint Gallery '99

Sources
Texas Transportation Institute, *1997 Urban Mobility Report* (College Station, Texas: Texas Transportation Institute, 1997).

Scott Thomas, "Population Projections for Leading Metros 1995 to 2020," *Bizjournal.com,* July 1998.

Scott Thomas, "Employment Growth By Market December 1989 to December 1998," *Bizjournal.com, Demographics Daily,* April 1999.

U.S. Bureau of the Census, *State Population Rankings Summary, 1995 to 2025* (Washington, D.C.: U.S. Department of Commerce, Bureau of the Census, Population Division, October 1996).

John Villani, "The Desired Zone," *Urban Land,* June 2000.

PROFILE: Charlotte, North Carolina
Transit Planning Guides Future Growth

Smart Growth Tools

⊙ Dedicated transit fund

⊙ *2025 Transit/Land-Use Plan*

⊙ Smart growth audit

⊙ Inclusive decision-making process

The Community

The city of Charlotte is located in south central North Carolina, midway between the Appalachian Mountains and the Atlantic Ocean and 240 miles northeast of Atlanta at the intersection of Interstates 77 and 85. A high quality of life and an expanding economy are helping to make Charlotte one of the fastest-growing cities in the United States. The Charlotte-Mecklenburg region owes its current makeup to relatively recent forces. A growing number of banking institutions, corporate enterprises, and other industries like printing/publishing and machinery are moving to or expanding in the region. Local business leaders include Bank of America, First Union Bank, U.S. Airways, Duke Energy, Microsoft, Transamerica, and TIAA CREF.

The Charlotte region encompasses the city of Charlotte and six surrounding towns—Davidson, Cornelius, Huntersville, Matthews, Mint Hill, and Pineville— each with its own land use authority. Since 1950, relatively liberal state annexation laws have allowed Charlotte to expand from 34.5 to more than 240 square miles, an increase of nearly 600 percent.

The Charlotte region is home to a number of universities and colleges, including the University of North Carolina (UNC)–Charlotte, Central Piedmont Community College, Gaston College, and Johnson C. Smith University. Three professional

A high quality of life and an expanding economy are helping to make Charlotte one of the fastest-growing cities in the United States.

With the addition of new high-quality down-town housing, the city of Charlotte is creating a 24-hour live, work, and play atmosphere.

sports teams have located in Charlotte since 1988: the National Basketball Association's Charlotte Hornets, the National Football League's Carolina Panthers, and the Women's National Basketball Association's Charlotte Sting. Two new sports venues, Ericsson Stadium and the Charlotte Coliseum, have been built in the past 15 years.

North of the city, the Catawba River and its system of constructed lakes—the largest of which is Lake Norman—provide recreational opportunities and some of the region's most expensive new housing. UNC-Charlotte and University Research Park are attracting newcomers to the northeast part of the city. The south and southeast sections of the region also are experiencing rapid growth along Independence Boulevard and the partially completed I-485 outer beltway.

THE CHARLOTTE REGION: FACTS AND FIGURES

⊙ Since the 1970s, Charlotte has positioned itself as the nation's second leading financial center, with approximately $774 billion in banking resources and two of the nation's top-25 banks (Bank of America and First Union) headquartered downtown.

⊙ Charlotte's reputation as a sleepy southern city offering a high quality of life has proven to be a magnet for business and industry.

⊙ Unemployment rates for the metropolitan area are lower than state and national rates.

⊙ Between 1980 and 2000, Mecklenburg County's population grew from 404,000 to 661,000. With this growth rate of 2.65 percent per year, Charlotte has moved in rank from the country's 50th largest city in 1974 to the 25th largest in 2000.

⊙ The seven-county metropolitan statistical area encompasses 3,390 square miles and has a population of 1.4 million.

Traffic congestion, loss of open space, and degraded air quality are some of the undesirable byproducts of the region's tremendous economic growth. Community leaders are taking proactive steps to ensure that future growth will not undermine the region's economy, quality of life, and environment.

Smart Growth Strategy

The smart growth dialogue now taking place in the Charlotte-Mecklenburg region builds upon years of work and the proactive stance the community has taken towards its future. Since 1994, the community has moved through a process involving conceptual development, public planning, legislative action, and an outside, unbiased assessment of how all the planning pieces may or may not fit together to actualize the conceptual vision.

In 1994, the Charlotte City Council and the Mecklenburg Board of County Commissioners adopted a vision for the future of their growing region based on transportation and development corridors extending from the city center. Charlotte-Mecklenburg's *2025 Transit/Land-Use Plan,* which was written in 1998, embraced this vision by defining five corridors where development of transportation infrastructure would be concentrated, thereby influencing land use patterns and regional growth.

Laura Simmons, a planner with the Charlotte-Mecklenburg Planning Commission, credits Mecklenberg Board of County Commissioners Chair Parks Helms and Charlotte Mayor Pat McCrory with bringing the community together under the rubric of smart growth in the late 1990s. The initiative that followed is a multiphase process. The first phase, completed in September 1999, includes a smart growth audit. Phase II, currently underway in mid-2000, includes a thorough review of the audit and subsequent recommendations for action by a community task force.

Smart Growth Tools

Dedicated Transit Fund

In November 1998, Mecklenburg County voters approved a referendum for a half-cent sales tax to fund the cost of new transit operations. The tax became effective on April 1, 1999, and is expected to generate an estimated $50 million annually, with infrastructure developments and land use policies phased in over a 25-year period. The Metropolitan Transit Commission (MTC) has been formed to coordinate transit operations on a countywide basis.

2025 Transit/Land-Use Plan

This Charlotte-Mecklenburg Planning Commission document addresses how and where future growth should be directed in accordance with the adopted "centers and corridors" vision. It proposes concentrating office centers near transit stations and focusing multifamily housing development along transportation corridors. To support this pattern of growth, the plan proposes establishing a bus rapid transit (BIT) system and developing rail technology along these corridors, as well as providing feeder bus services to the "wedges" (the areas between the corridors). Total costs—capital expenditures, operations, and maintenance—for the proposed transit system will be $1.09 billion over 25 years. Benefits for this same time period are estimated at $72 million.

Smart Growth Audit

The smart growth audit represents Phase I of the region's formal smart growth initiative. The Charlotte-Mecklenburg Planning Commission initiated this audit as a means of evaluating the current policies and plans relative to smart growth, and identifying "gaps" where more work needs to be done. The main objective of the smart growth audit, conducted by the Columbia, Maryland–based urban design and land use planning firm LDR. International, Inc., was to provide the community with a structured, objective evaluation of how it is promoting smart growth principles. The first task of the audit team was to evaluate the various definitions of smart growth and formulate a working set of principles that expressed the ideals of the Charlotte-Mecklenburg community.

Addressing the challenge of formulating a smart growth strategy, the audit team reports, "The stage of growth in a community, the degree to which the local economy is expanding and diversifying (or not), the number and size of the various local jurisdictions, the scope of powers that a state delegates to its local jurisdictions, the degree to which interjurisdictional cooperation is already in place, the political realities and civic culture, and the quality of governance and administration all will bear directly on smart growth possibilities."

To evaluate the principles of smart growth, the audit team reviewed public plans and documents, interviewed key stakeholders, and reviewed local decision-making processes. The audit team presented its findings and recommendations in report form to the Charlotte-Mecklenburg Planning Commission. Its six major recommendations were:

1) Streamline development codes and review processes,

2) Establish proactive policies and powers to implement centers and corridors,

3) Plan ahead for the needs of the future,

4) Establish a more thorough planning database and development tracking system,

5) Conduct a fiscal impact analysis of the outcome of current plans and policies, and

6) Develop a unified open space environmental and parks strategy.

Inclusive Decision-Making Process

Phase II of the community's smart growth initiative began upon completion of the smart growth audit, when the Charlotte-Mecklenburg Planning Liaison Committee appointed a 32-member citizen task force to review the audit in detail and assist the planning commission staff in identifying major priority initiatives. The members were chosen to represent the full spectrum of interests in the region, thereby building consensus from the early stages of the smart growth initiative.

Information Contacts

Robert Morgan
Vice President
Public Policy
Charlotte Chamber of Commerce
330 South Tyron Street
Charlotte, North Carolina 28232
704-378-1300

Martin Crampton
Planning Director
Charlotte-Mecklenburg Planning Commission
600 East Fourth Street, Eighth Floor
Charlotte, North Carolina 28202
704-336-5721

Resources

Web Sites
Charlotte Chamber of Commerce   **www.charlottechamber.com**
Charlotte-Mecklenburg Web site,   **www.charmeck.nc.us**
   the official government site for the
   city of Charlotte and Mecklenburg
   County, North Carolina

Sources
Charlotte-Mecklenburg Planning Commission, *2025 Transit/Land-Use Plan*. Available at www.ci.charlottte.nc.us.

"Charlotte Metropolitan Area," in *ULI Market Profiles 1999: North America* (Washington, D.C.: ULI–the Urban Land Institute, 1999).

LDR. International, Inc., "A Smart Growth Audit for Charlotte-Mecklenburg County," submitted to the Charlotte-Mecklenburg Planning Commission, September 2, 1999. Available at www.charmeck.nc.us/ciplanning/index.htm.

Montgomery County, Maryland
Comprehensive Growth Management Policies Put into Practice

Smart Growth Tools

⊙ Transportation-supported development

⊙ Community livability programs

⊙ Inclusionary housing requirements

⊙ Open space conservation measures

⊙ Inclusive decision-making processes

The Community

Montgomery County, Maryland, lies on the northwestern boundary of the District of Columbia and is bordered on its western edge by the Potomac River. Once primarily agricultural, the county began suburbanizing in the 1890s with the development of Chevy Chase and other communities connected by trolley lines to Washington, D.C. The tremendous expansion of the Washington metropolitan area following World War II quickly spread into Montgomery and other close-in counties in Maryland and Virginia, turning sedate older communities such as Bethesda and Silver Spring into bustling regional centers. The county's population currently numbers 855,000 and is growing by 1 to 2 percent a year.

Montgomery County today is as much urban as suburban in character. The county has attracted significant economic growth, much of it focused in high-tech industries. Almost 60 percent of its residents work within the county and development is becoming intensified in regional commercial, employment, and residential centers. The county government (Maryland's counties act much as municipalities do in other states) is funding a new conference center and several arts centers. The county's excellent educational and park systems continue to make it one of the most desirable residential areas in the Washington, D.C., region.

MONTGOMERY COUNTY: FACTS AND FIGURES

⊙ **Montgomery County is the most populous county in Maryland.**

⊙ **The median household income in 1999 was $71,930, up from $66,085 just three years earlier.**

⊙ **Housing prices average $362,000 for new single-family houses and $235,000 for resale houses.**

⊙ **The county's population has become more diverse, especially in the last two decades. In 1999, 13 percent of its residents were African American, 11 percent Asian, and almost 9 percent Hispanic.**

⊙ **Montgomery County provides 90 percent of Maryland's high-wage (over $50,000) jobs.**

⊙ **Employment has increased steadily by 3.4 percent annually, outpacing population growth. Jobs grew from 465,970 in 1990 to 503,000 in 1999, primarily in the private sector.**

Smart Growth Strategy

The county has earned a reputation over more than 60 years for comprehensive, imaginative, and aggressive planning and growth management. Indeed, says Robert Harris, an attorney with Wilkes Artis Chartered, "the county was into smart growth before smart growth was cool." The county's planning processes began in 1927 with the formation of the Maryland–National Capital Park and Planning Commission, a bicounty planning, zoning, and park acquisition agency. Montgomery County adopted a home rule charter in 1948 and designated a county planning board as part of the park and planning commission.

County planning efforts are grounded in a general plan approved in 1964, which lays out a development pattern of "wedges and corridors." The wedges were to be reserved as low-density rural lands, with development corridors centered on the I-270 and U.S. 29 highways. In the 1970s and 1980s, development along the corridors was reinforced by the extension of 18.5 miles of Washington Metrorail service along both corridors. The conservation of green wedges was assisted in 1980 by the designation of a farmland preservation area in the northern third of the county. The county's basic development strategy remains focused on intensifying development along the corridors and increasing the use of public transit while conserving substantial areas as open space. As Richard Tustian, the county's long-time (now retired) planning director observes, "much of the county's planning in recent years has focused on refinement and closer-grained articulation of the basic wedges and corridor concept."

SMART GROWTH PLAYERS

⊙ **Multiple Stakeholder Groups.** Montgomery County's generally inclusive decision-making processes have developed a well-honed constituency for smart growth policies, including several major citizen groups and an array of special interest organizations focused on county development policies. The business community, including developers and homebuilders, occasionally indicates unhappiness with some county policies that restrain development, but many representatives of private interests serve on the numerous committees and task forces that generate consensus for county programs and actions. Over the past decade especially, business and citizen groups have clashed over issues such as a new highway corridor and impact fees. The Silver Spring revitalization program, for example, championed public/private development efforts over the wishes of some neighborhood groups. The "players" in Montgomery County, in other words, tend to constitute the entire community.

⊙ **Action in Montgomery (AIM).** AIM is an advocacy group composed of ecumenical faith-based institutions that is working on affordable housing and elder care issues in the county.

⊙ **The State of Maryland.** The state declared itself a new player in smart growth in 1996 when it adopted smart growth legislation. The state's nationally recognized smart growth program directs state investments, such as funding for roads, sewers, schools, and other public investments, to "designated growth areas." The smart growth legislation puts the state in partnership with counties and municipalities to direct development in ways that promote fiscal responsibility and community livability. For a detailed description of one new element of this legislation, see "Maryland's Building Rehabilitation Code Program" on page 140.

The county also has adopted a battery of other growth management techniques, including a requirement for proof of adequate public facilities as a condition of development approval, a transfer of development rights (TDR) program to compensate landowners in the farmland preservation area, an inclusionary housing program added to other housing programs for low- and moderate-income families, a redevelopment program to revive the Silver Spring downtown area, incentives for transit-oriented development and transportation demand management, and increasing attention to providing the cultural infrastructure central to the livability of an urban community.

Smart Growth Tools

Transportation-Supported Development

Since the Washington Metrorail system was launched in the 1970s, the county has encouraged transit-supportive patterns of development in response to the mounting traffic congestion experienced in every growing suburban area. The "wedges and corridors" general plan established the overall framework for this policy and subsequent preparation of community and detailed sector plans has built on that foundation. The county consistently has supported higher-density development and redevelopment around rail stations and along major highways, sometimes over the objections of nearby residents.

Montgomery County has established an aggressive density-bonus, mixed-use zoning program to encourage growth in designated areas, including near transit stations.

COURTESY OF THE WASHINGTON METROPOLITAN AREA TRANSIT AUTHORITY

Two manifestations of the county's interest in promoting intensive development around rail stations are its support of Bethesda's transformation from a sleepy community commercial crossroads into a regional business center and the redevelopment of the old declining downtown of Silver Spring, both centered on Metrorail stations. County officials, working collaboratively with the transit authority and private developers, established design parameters and approved density increases for mixed-use development over the centrally located rail station in Bethesda. The county followed up with an aggressive density-bonus mixed-use zoning program that produced significant public amenities during a period of strong office and commercial development. Private redevelopment continues apace, as county-financed parking garages and pedestrian bridges and streetscape improvements funded through a business improvement district have completely recast the Bethesda scene.

At the other end of the Metrorail Red Line, in the eastern part of the county, the Silver Spring business district is being reshaped by major development around the rail station (and multimodal center) and by county-sponsored redevelopment of an old downtown area that had been in decline for decades. County officials pushed redevelopment efforts by assembling land, promising infrastructure improvements, and sponsoring a ULI Advisory Services panel to recommend a workable redevelopment process. After several false starts and considerable controversy, the county has selected a developer who is constructing the first phase of a mixed-use retail, office, and entertainment center. A similar, smaller-scale redevelopment program is underway in the county seat of Rockville.

The county also continues to promote development around other rail stations, even to the point of relaxing traffic standards of service in station areas. As of mid-2000, it is beginning development of a conference center at one station and is significantly expanding an arts center at another. In addition, the county has initiated a number of effective transportation demand management programs. In areas already affected by traffic congestion, it has worked with employers to formulate programs to reduce the use of single-occupant automobiles by promoting car- and vanpools, issuing transit passes, and providing shuttle buses to nearby rail transit stations.

Community Livability Programs

While county policies promote intensive development in certain locations, they also protect established neighborhoods, encourage high-quality design of new neighborhoods, provide below-market rate housing, and establish a high standard for public services that benefit residents. As early as 1973, the county adopted an adequate facilities ordinance meant to ensure that roads, water and sewer service, and other community facilities were capable of serving prospective development. Tied to the county's capital improvement program, which schedules new capital construction, the adequacy requirements have shut down development in some areas until the capacities of public facilities—chiefly roads—have been expanded or mitigated through transportation demand programs. More often, developers are persuaded to "contribute" to facility expansions, in some cases assisted by special county funding arrangements. Nevertheless, many residents see the ordinance as the front line of county efforts to reduce traffic and other impacts on established and developing neighborhoods.

Although school and park capacities also are part of the adequate facilities test, they seldom pose a problem since the county has maintained a steady stream of investment in new or refurbished schools, parkland acquisition, and construction of recreational facilities. These facilities are prized by county residents as central elements of community livability.

Inclusionary Housing Requirements

To offset high housing prices generated by the county's residential desirability—and, some say, the restrictive regulatory climate—the county has initiated programs to provide housing for low- and moderate-income residents. The centerpiece of this effort has been an inclusionary housing requirement: all residential developments of 50 or more units must include a proportion of moderate-cost housing. In return, a sliding scale of density bonuses is awarded to relieve the developer's financial burden of providing such housing. Strict design standards mitigate against identifying the units as lower-cost homes and resale restrictions keep the housing available to lower-income residents. Such county housing programs have produced more than 10,700 scattered-site below-market housing units, including 1,500 units purchased by the county's housing authority and nonprofit housing providers to be rented to very low-income households.

Open Space Conservation Measures

The county's subdivision regulations, backed up by state regulations, regularly have required setbacks from streams, tree conservation, and minimum open space standards for new development. The park and planning commission's long-term commitment to parkland acquisition has created over 28,000 acres of

Since Montgomery County's transfer of development rights (TDR) program was started in 1980, more than 35,000 acres of agricultural and environmentally sensitive lands have been conserved.

park and recreation space in the county. Residents also enjoy access to the northern one-third of the county zoned for minimum 25-acre lots to preserve farmland. Long-term farmland preservation is ensured by the transfer of development rights (TDR) program, through which developers purchase and transfer farmland development rights to obtain rights to higher-density development in down-county "receiving" areas designated in area master plans. Since the program began in 1980, 35,000 acres have been preserved. In addition, Maryland's new rural legacy program—a component of the state's smart growth initiative—is supplementing its existing program for purchasing open space development easements by pumping funds into conservation of environmentally sensitive open space.

The drawback to the TDR program, says attorney Robert Harris, is that many designated receiving zones have been shut down for development by the county's adequate public facilities requirements and by neighborhood opposition to intensified development. He cites a 15-year moratorium on new housing in a major highway corridor, as well as a general shortage of areas willing to accept transfers that would result in higher-density development.

Inclusive Decision-Making Processes

The county's growth has received constant attention from elected officials and civic leaders since early in the 20th century. Montgomery County traditionally has been home to many public servants who, with other residents, strongly support the pursuit of "good government" policies. Over many years, its planning program has been replete with task forces and study committees of all kinds, and residents consistently back strong public management of the development process.

Former Planning Director Richard Tustian is proud of the breadth of support for county growth management efforts, but points out that the lack of a regional development strategy has diluted the ability of the county to control the impacts of development, such as traffic. In particular, he notes that the "Balkanized jurisdictions have no way to achieve a workable distribution of growth throughout the region." As a result, for example, traffic from other counties is affecting county policies for controlling congestion.

Information Contacts

Elizabeth Davison
Director
Montgomery County Government
Department of Housing & Community Affairs
100 Maryland Avenue, Fourth Floor
Rockville, Maryland 20850
240-777-3600

Robert Harris
Vice President
Wilkes Artis, Chartered
3 Bethesda Metro Center
Suite 800
Bethesda, Maryland 20814
301-654-7800

Resources

Montgomery County, Maryland	**www.co.mo.md.us**
Montgomery County Planning Board	**www.mc-mncppc.org**
Maryland Department of Planning	**www.mdp.md.us**

Silicon Valley, California
Smart Programs Guide Growth in Explosive Economy

Smart Growth Tools

⊙ Transit-oriented development corridors

⊙ Urban growth boundaries

⊙ Housing Action Coalition

⊙ Land supply inventory

The Community

Located 45 minutes southeast of San Francisco, Silicon Valley lies nestled between the Santa Cruz Mountains and the East Bay foothills. This rapidly growing area is generally defined as the 15 cities within Santa Clara County, the three southernmost cities of Alameda County (Fremont, Newark, and Union City), and the three southernmost cities in San Mateo County (Palo Alto, Menlo Park, and Redwood City). In the last two decades, the valley, which represents more than one-third of the Bay Area's households and jobs, has seen its population grow from 1.6 million to 2.2 million people.

Prior to the 1950s, Silicon Valley was largely agricultural, with a strong dependence on fruit crops. The establishment of Stanford Industrial Park and IBM's research center in San Jose during the mid-1950s—and the invention of the microprocessor in 1972—changed the course of the region, as technology-related companies began taking root and flourishing there. Today, Silicon Valley is known throughout the world for its concentration of technology-based companies, talent,

SILICON VALLEY: FACTS AND FIGURES

⊙ The Association of Bay Area Governments (ABAG) estimates that the number of Silicon Valley residents increased by 36 percent between 1990 and 2000, while employment in the valley grew 48 percent during this same period. The valley's employment growth is projected to be double the increase in the number of households (36 percent versus 17 percent) by 2020.

⊙ Silicon Valley housing prices rose 46.2 percent between 1995 and 1999 (compared with 34.2 percent in the entire Bay Area during the same period).

⊙ Speeds during peak-hour commutes in the San Jose metropolitan area are slower than those in New York City and Chicago.

⊙ Mass transit does not play a significant role in Silicon Valley because of the predominantly low-density character of the area's development and the relatively low level of investment in transit. Santa Clara County has an initiative to provide significant sales tax funding for several new light-rail lines, expanded Caltrain commuter rail service, and a commuter rail link to the Bay Area Rapid Transit (BART) system in Alameda County.

Silicon Valley, nestled between the Santa Cruz Mountains and the East Bay foothills, is home to more than one-third of the San Francisco Bay Area's households and jobs.

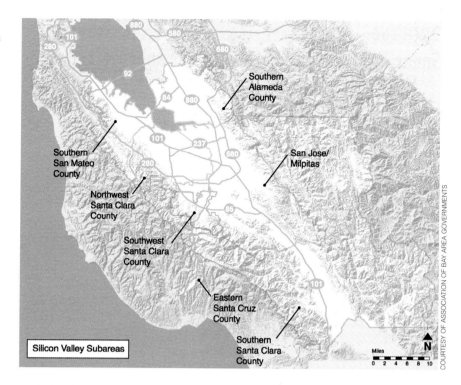

capital, universities, and entrepreneurial spirit. Fueled by the technology sector, the region has experienced unprecedented levels of employment growth. Since 1994, more than 250,000 new jobs were created in Silicon Valley. While the pace of growth is projected to slow, forecasters estimate another 200,000 new jobs will be added in the next decade. This exuberant growth has some negative impacts: employers are finding it increasingly difficult to recruit and retain workers because of limited housing choices and high costs, and the environment is being degraded by extended commutes and increased pressure to develop open space and farmland. The question of how to balance continued economic growth and development with environmental, social equity, and community preservation goals is critical to the region's future.

Smart Growth Strategy

Following a period of unmanaged, leapfrogging development and sprawl between 1950 and 1970, Silicon Valley cities and counties have implemented plans, policies, and programs aimed at promoting land use decisions that are economically feasible, environmentally sustainable, and socially equitable. Today, the region is home to some of the more innovative and progressive local efforts to curb urban sprawl, revitalize existing communities, and preserve open space.

San Jose began implementing smart growth policies in the 1970s, with the establishment of urban service areas, infill development incentives, designated land for high-density development, and downtown and neighborhood revitalization plans. In the 1980s, the city began reserving strategic locations for economic development and establishing "nonurban hillside" designations to avoid further degradation of the area's environment. San Jose continued to enhance its progressive smart growth tools by adopting general plan policies that encouraged transit-oriented mixed-use development. In addition, the city set a precedent for creating community-based specific plans to recycle land into livable, pedestrian-friendly neighborhoods. Toward the late 1990s, San Jose led the region in creating a greenline/urban growth boundary.

In 1979, David Packard (one of the founders of the Hewlett-Packard Company) and other high-tech industry leaders created the Silicon Valley Manufacturing

Group (SVMG) as a constructive, coalition-building force for Silicon Valley. Working with business, civic, and environmental leaders, as well as government officials, the group has tackled major public policy issues affecting the economic health and quality of life in Silicon Valley. The group advocates improved housing, transportation, land use, and environmental quality at all levels of government—from neighborhoods to federal agencies—through its influence and the financial backing of local businesses and community partnerships. SVMG works on housing issues by involving 150 groups and individuals in the Housing Action Coalition.

In 1995, the Metropolitan Transportation Commission (MTC), the Bay Area's transportation planning and financing agency, initiated the Transportation for Livable Communities (TLC) grant program to support plans and projects that strengthen the link between transportation, community goals, and land use. Among other things, the program aims to support small-scale transportation projects—such as streetscape improvements and transit-, pedestrian-, and bicycle-oriented developments—that make a significant contribution to a community's livability. MTC allocates $9 million annually from funds made available by the federal Transportation Equity Act for the 21st Century (TEA-21) for planning grants and capital grants. Projects in the early or conceptual stage of development are eligible for up to $50,000 each; grants for capital improvements range from $150,000 to $2 million per project. These are just a few of the many initiatives being used to advance smart growth in the region.

The Bay Area Alliance for Sustainable Development, a multistakeholder group established in 1997, has facilitated a region-wide dialogue and prepared a draft "Compact for a Sustainable Bay Area." The draft compact identifies key regional challenges and recommends a package of ten strategic commitments to meet those challenges. The goal of this initiative is to reach broad consensus on a set of actions that will move the Bay Area toward a more sustainable future.

In an effort to draw on the success of these initiatives—and other effective programs from other regions—ABAG, MTC, and the Bay Area Air Quality Management District (BAAQMD) launched the Partnership for Smart Growth in 1999. This group plans to use a comprehensive inventory of smart growth policies that have the potential to be replicated within the region and nationwide. It also will investigate fiscal and other barriers to more sustainable local land uses and compatible transportation investments, and will identify potential local, regional, and statewide funding programs and other incentives that could be used to promote smarter growth at the local level. The partnership will employ a set of visualization tools

SMART GROWTH PLAYERS

⊙ **The Partnership for Smart Growth (a collaboration between the Association of Bay Area Governments, the Metropolitan Transportation Commission and the Bay Area Air Quality Management District).**

⊙ **The Silicon Valley Manufacturing Group (SVMG).**

⊙ **The Greenbelt Alliance.**

⊙ **The Bay Area Transportation and Land Use Coalition.**

⊙ **Santa Clara County, San Mateo County, Alameda County, and the city of San Jose.**

⊙ **The Bay Area Alliance for Sustainable Development.**

⊙ **The ULI San Francisco District Council.**

and development scenarios to demonstrate the potential impacts smart growth actions could have on the region's growth pattern. It also will identify strategies that can be implemented by cities and counties to strengthen the link between land use, transportation, community vitality, social equity, and environmental preservation.

Complementing the success of these initiatives, five regional agencies in the Bay Area are beginning work on a smart growth strategy that would institutionalize a new approach to planning for future growth in the region. This two-year effort will work toward two goals: land use changes and an incentive plan that are supported by local governments, and a set of smart growth projections to guide implementation policies for the regional agencies and the development of regional plans, including a regional transportation plan.

The agencies directing this effort include ABAG, MTC, BAAQMD, the Bay Conservation and Development Commission, and the Regional Water Quality Control Board. They will be contributing funding and staffing to match a grant from the U.S. Environmental Protection Agency (EPA). Advising partners include the steering committee of the Bay Area Alliance for Sustainable Development, the Bay Area Transportation and Land Use Coalition, and the ULI San Francisco District Council.

Following a series of public workshops and technical analysis, maps within each Bay Area subregion will define where and how future growth should be accommodated, together with necessary changes to current land use policies and transportation investment strategies. The effort also will identify and implement needed fiscal and regulatory incentives to support smart growth land use decisions.

Smart Growth Tools

Transit-Oriented Development Corridors

As a means to achieve key general plan objectives, the city of San Jose has implemented a "transit-oriented development corridors" policy to promote compact development along major transportation corridors and hubs. The city's general plan lists six key transit-oriented development corridors where higher intensities of development are encouraged. Transit-oriented development corridors help achieve vigorous economic growth, more affordable housing opportunities, shelter for a growing population, increased transportation capacity through increased transit use, efficient delivery of urban services, and a solid fiscal base for the city.

These corridors are generally suitable for higher residential densities, more intensive nonresidential uses, and mixed uses. The corridors are centered along existing or planned light-rail transit (LRT) lines and/or major bus routes. They are intended to include sites within approximately 500 feet of the right-of-way of the corridor's central transportation facility or within approximately 2,000 feet of an existing or planned LRT station.

Because of the varied character of development found along the city's transit corridors, two types of appropriate residential development have been designated:

Urban Transit Corridor Residential. This designation is intended for sites located in the "downtown core" and "frame" areas or within 2,000 feet of LRT stations in other intensely developed parts of the city. Development should be either wholly residential or residential over commercial uses on the first two floors. Densities generally should exceed 45 dwelling units per acre. This category is intended to expand the potential for residential development with convenient access to major job centers and to create new consumer markets in appropriate areas.

Suburban Transit Corridor Residential. This designation is intended for suburban areas within 2,000 feet of LRT stations. Densities should average at least 20 dwelling units per acre. Wholly residential projects or those with street-level commercial uses and residences on upper floors are permitted. Neighborhood-serving commercial uses also are permitted in freestanding buildings, provided that they are zoned and built as part of a residential project, have a clear functional and architectural relationship to the residential buildings, and are located along a pedestrian pathway system with convenient links to the LRT station and nearby housing.

The program already has proven to be a great success, with more than 10,000 housing units built or approved by the city of San Jose since its establishment.

The Villa Torino housing project helped transform a once blighted neighborhood in San Jose into a vibrant community.

Urban Growth Boundaries

Urban growth boundaries (UGBs) are a planning strategy aimed at minimizing urban sprawl, protecting open space, and strengthening neighborhoods and cities. A UGB is an officially mapped and adopted line that separates an urban area from its surrounding greenbelt open lands, including farms, watersheds, and parks. Urban growth boundaries are set for significant periods of time—typically 20 years or more—to accommodate future growth and to discourage speculation at the urban or suburban fringe. Eleven Silicon Valley communities have adopted UGBs with the intent of maintaining their identities, protecting open space and farmland, saving tax dollars, and strengthening downtowns.

To be an effective tool, long-term UGBs (containing a 20-year supply of available land for urban development) are reviewed periodically to determine if there is a need to revise the boundaries. Typically, five years after the UGB is designated, an initial review of growth projections is conducted. Ten years following delineation of a UGB, a comprehensive review occurs in order to reestablish a 20-year supply of land within the UGB. "San Jose believes that to manage growth, development needs to be directed to the 'right' place," explains Laurel Prevetti, principal planner, city of San Jose. "Infill strategies and urban growth boundaries work together to direct growth in desired locations."

Housing Action Coalition

In 1993, a diverse group of public and private organizations and interests— whose common goal is to provide affordable, well-constructed, and appropriately located housing in Santa Clara County—formed the Housing Action Coalition. The group uses its collective voice to advocate for housing proposals whose merit it determines through a set of criteria that includes location, density, affordability, and design. In addition to this advocacy role, the coalition educates city councils, planning commissions, and community groups about housing and related issues, and supports relevant litigation. A CEO-level Housing Leadership Council assists the coalition with a series of initiatives aimed at developing substantive solutions to the valley's housing crisis. The group also tackles transportation issues, addressing the relationship between transportation, housing, and the environment. As of mid-2000, the coalition has either helped or directly resulted in the approval of 71 housing projects, representing 24,000 new homes in 16 different Silicon Valley cities. For more information on this group, see "The Housing Action Coalition of Santa Clara County's Project Endorsement Program" on page 140.

Land Supply Inventory

The Silicon Valley Manufacturing Group and the Greenbelt Alliance, the San Francisco Bay area's leading land conservation organization, have forged a strong partnership to radically increase housing production within Silicon Valley in a manner that addresses both business and environmental concerns. In 1999, the two groups released the third comprehensive inventory of vacant and underused land available for housing development within the valley's 21 core cities. *Housing Solutions for Silicon Valley* was funded by the ABAG and the Santa Clara Valley Transportation Authority. The report assesses the magnitude of both the current land supply and potential housing yield in Silicon Valley, based on current local land use policy and market conditions. The first two inventories spurred the development of thousands of homes.

Information Contacts

Faye Beverett
Page Street Properties LLC
3 Embarcadero Center, Suite 1150
San Francisco, California 941111-4042
415-398-2266
Fax: 415-398-2272
E-mail: pagestr@aol.com

Brian Kirking
Senior Planner
Association of Bay Area Governments
P.O. Box 2050
Oakland, California 94604-2050
510-464-7996
Fax: 510-464-7970
E-mail: Briank@abag.ca.gov

Resources

Association of Bay Area Governments	**www.abag.ca.gov**
Silicon Valley Manufacturing Group	**www.svmg.org**
Santa Clara County	**www.claraweb.co.santa-clara.ca.us.**
City of San Jose	**www.ci.san-jose.ca.us**

PART THREE

Smart Development Case Studies

ULI has a history of providing best practice case studies for various types of development projects. This tradition continues as ULI seeks to elevate the smart growth dialogue by providing examples of projects that reflect smart growth characteristics. The 19 case studies included here are listed under four categories: infill development, brownfield redevelopment, inner-ring development, and suburban development. Each smart development case study includes a description of some of the project's smart growth characteristics and some of the challenges that it overcame to be built. Smart growth characteristics that are not highlighted in the case study are noted in the summary matrix on page 45.

Selecting development examples that reflect smart growth is not an easy undertaking. The debate over what is and what is not smart growth development is ongoing. ULI chose these 19 case studies for the *Smart Growth Tool Kit* because they incorporate many of the features that ULI and others consider fundamental elements of smart growth. These features can be found in development projects located in urban, inner-ring suburban, and suburban areas. They are:

⊙ Mixed-use development,

⊙ Master-planned communities,

⊙ Town centers,

⊙ Downtown revitalization,

- Conservation design,

- Traditional neighborhood design,

- Transit-oriented design,

- Pedestrian-oriented design,

- Open space protection/environmental features,

- Adaptive use/historical preservation,

- Affordable housing,

- Public/private partnerships, and

- Collaborative planning.

Most projects face some barriers to their development, and projects that reflect smart growth characteristics are no exception. In fact, many developers have noted that a project that achieves the objectives and incorporates the features of smart growth can face even more challenges than conventional development. Some of the common challenges that are highlighted in the case studies include:

- High construction costs,

- Financing complications,

- Infrastructure deficits,

- Parking limitations,

- Political opposition,

- Public opposition,

- Need for public education,

- Regulatory barriers,

- Site constraints, and

- Untested markets.

The following 19 case studies demonstrate that smart growth projects take various shapes and sizes—from small-scale residential to large-scale mixed-use projects. But regardless of their shape or size, each case study provides examples of common smart growth features and challenges. The following case studies highlight those common features and the challenges to their successful implementation.

Smart Growth Characteristics Matrix

Smart Growth Projects	Mixed-Use Development	Master-Planned Community	Town Center	Downtown Revitalization	Conservation Design	Traditional Neighborhood Design	Transit-Oriented Design	Pedestrian-Oriented Design	Open Space Protection/ Environmental Features	Adaptive Use/ Historic Preservation	Affordable Housing	Public/Private Partnership	Collaborative Planning
Infill Development													
Courthouse Hill, Arlington, Virginia		✦				●		●	●				
Denver Dry Goods Building, Denver, Colorado	●			✦				✦		●	✦	●	
Downtown Park, Bellevue, Washington				●				✦	●			●	✦
East Lake Commons, Decatur, Georgia					●	●		✦	✦				●
MCI Center, Washington, D.C.				●			●	●	✦			●	
Brownfield Redevelopment													
The Can Company, Baltimore, Maryland	✦			✦				✦	✦	●		●	●
Pearl Court Apartments, Portland, Oregon				✦			●	✦	●		●	●	✦
Washington's Landing, Pittsburgh, Pennsylvania	●			✦				✦	●			●	
Inner-Ring Development													
Addison Circle, Addison, Texas	●	✦	✦			●	✦	✦	✦		✦	●	✦
Bethesda Row, Bethesda, Maryland	●		●	✦		✦	●	●				●	
Harbor Town, Memphis, Tennessee	●	✦				●		✦	●		✦		
Phillips Place, Charlotte, North Carolina	✦		●			✦		●				✦	
Suburban Development													
Bonita Bay, Bonita Springs, Florida		✦			●			✦	●				✦
Fairview Village, Fairview, Oregon	✦	✦				✦		●	✦			✦	●
Orenco Station, Hillsboro, Oregon	✦	✦	●			✦	●	●	✦			✦	✦
Prairie Crossing, Grayslake, Illinois	✦	✦			●		✦	●	●				●
Promenade at Westlake, Thousand Oaks, California			✦					●				✦	●
Rancho Santa Margarita, Rancho Santa Margarita, California	●	●	✦		✦			✦	●		✦		
Reston Town Center, Reston, Virginia	✦	✦	●			●		✦	✦	✦			

● Project characteristics that are highlighted in the case study.

✦ Project characteristics that are not featured in the case study.

CASE STUDY: Courthouse Hill
Arlington, Virginia

Smart Growth Characteristics

⊙ Transit- and pedestrian-oriented design

⊙ Traditional neighborhood design

Smart Growth Challenges

⊙ Site constraints

⊙ Regulatory barriers

The Project

Courthouse Hill is a 202-unit infill project of townhouses and mid-rise condominiums located in Arlington, Virginia, just one block from Washington, D.C., Metrorail's Courthouse station. Although the project is surrounded by a mix of high-rise office and residential buildings, as well as low-rise housing to the south, the developer, Eakin/Youngentob Associates, avoided the tower-in-the-park solution for this 4.6-acre site. Instead, inspired by Washington-area 18th- and 19th-century rowhouse neighborhoods, the developer focused on creating a pedestrian-oriented neighborhood that takes advantage of the site's urban context.

The result, completed in April 1997, is a complex of 69 three-story townhomes and 133 condominiums in a mix of four-, five-, and six-story structures, woven together by a network of landscaped parks and pathways. At 29 units per acre for the townhouses and 87 units per acre for the condominiums, the project has achieved densities greater than those usually reached by comparable projects. At the same time, because of the high level of building and site detailing—everything from tree-lined brick walkways to molded cornices—the project sold out rapidly and commanded above-average per-square-foot prices.

Courthouse Hill's proximity to urban amenities was a major selling point for potential residents, who placed a high value on being within walking distance of transit, restaurants, movie theaters, shops, and offices. According to architect Chris Lessard, principal of Lessard Architectural Group, "The person we were trying to appeal to is the young person or empty nester who is interested in a vibrant street life. So in our design we sought to create a sense of community that related to and enhanced the surrounding urban environment." Adds developer Bob Youngentob, "Our target market was not the type that desires living in a gated community. People want to feel a part of a neighborhood."

The market response to Courthouse Hill was very positive. Nearly all of the 204 units were sold in less than 18 months, a rate of about 11 units per month. Prices ranged from $115,000 to $280,000 for the condominiums and from $280,000 to $350,000 for the townhouses. Twenty-eight of the 133 condominium units were designated as affordable for-sale housing, fulfilling county requirements.

Smart Growth Characteristics

Transit- and Pedestrian-Oriented Design
The project's pedestrian-oriented design strategy included placing building entrances on the street and relegating parking to the interior of the site. Like their 18th- and 19th-century townhouse antecedents, the Courthouse Hill structures are

Because of the high level of building and site detailing, this high-density project (29 units per acre for townhouses and 87 units per acre for the condominiums) sold out rapidly and commanded above-average per-square-foot prices.

set close to the street, just 14.5 feet from the curb. Entrances to the individual town-homes are raised, both for privacy and to accommodate tucked-under parking.

The configuration of open space also helps to establish a pedestrian orientation. The developer built a one-half-acre public park on the southern edge of the project that links it with a recreation center across the street and the neighborhood beyond. Landscaped pathways thread their way from the park through Court-house Hill, connecting to the Metrorail station and the urban core to the north. These walkways are pledged to public use through the mechanism of a pedestrian access easement. Both sidewalks and internal walkways are paved in brick and illuminated by lantern and period streetlights, further recalling the project's urban antecedents.

Traditional Neighborhood Design

Although built by one developer, the townhouse facades at Courthouse Hill are varied, echoing the eclectic mix typical of older neighborhoods built one house at a time. The highly detailed brick facades are federal period in style, with pedi-mented doorways, arched window heads, and strong cornice lines. Dormer windows punctuate the steeply pitched roofs. At the street level, raised entry stoops with metal railings provide a rhythm and a unifying element for the facades. Each townhouse has an integral two-car garage, accessed via an interior driveway.

The condominium buildings are a less literal translation of period architecture, but employ the same finish materials as the townhouses. As is the case with the town-houses, the elevations are highly articulated, with painted wood details contrasting with brick facades. Recessed balconies further modulate the elevations. Roofs are pitched and accented with dormers and gables of varying sizes.

Smart Growth Challenges

Site Constraints

The Courthouse Hill site was a difficult one; the area was urban, yet not particularly friendly to pedestrians. The site borders high rises on one side and single-family residences on another, and slopes 35 feet from end to end. Although well-located, the cleared site had remained vacant for ten years before Eakin/Youngentob purchased it.

Parking for the condominium buildings is provided in below-grade structures. To deal with the site's 35-foot elevation gradient, the developer regraded relatively level driveways, and set some of the townhouse garages partially below grade.

Regulatory Barriers

The site originally was zoned for high-rise development. To Eakin/Youngentob, this was exactly the opposite of what it needed. What was required, the developer and architect reasoned, was a greater connection to the site's context (not the lesser engagement implied by high-rise development), a reestablishment of the urban pattern, and a pedestrian scale. Notes architect Lessard, "Above five stories, people start to feel disconnected from the street level." The low-/mid-rise solution also provides a much-needed break in the skyline, and does not block light and sun from surrounding streets.

As a first step in integrating the site with its context, the developer and architect decided to bridge the differences in massing of the surrounding structures. Lessard notes, "The layout of housing units on the site sought to create a 'layering effect' that ties the project into the neighborhood fabric." This was achieved by stepping down in height from the high-rise office/retail center and Metro station to the north to the low-rise housing to the south. The taller condominium buildings step from six to five to four stories, and the townhomes complete the layering effect by establishing a three-story profile adjacent to the community park and existing residential neighborhood to the south.

Project Data

Land Uses

Site area	4.6 acres
Total dwelling units	202
Townhouses	69
Condominiums	133
Gross density	43.9 units per acre
Net density	69.7 units per acre
Average lot size	902 square feet
Parking	345 spaces
Parking ratio	1.71 spaces/unit

Land Use Plan

Use	Acres	Percent of Site
Residential	2.1	46%
Recreation/amenities	0.7	15%
Roads/parking	0.8	17%
Open space	1.0	22%
Total	4.6	100%

Information Contact

Eakin/Youngentob Associates
1000 Wilson Boulevard, Suite 2720
Arlington, Virginia 22209
703-525-5565

CASE STUDY: Denver Dry Goods Building
Denver, Colorado

Smart Growth Characteristics

⊙ Mixed-use development

⊙ Adaptive use

⊙ Public/private partnership

Smart Growth Challenges

⊙ Financing and leasing complications

⊙ Infrastructure deficits

The Project

This project is the adaptive use of the historic Denver Dry Goods Building, built in 1888. The six-story structure has been renovated to create affordable and market-rate housing, retail, and office space. The 350,000-square-foot building was sub-divided into condominium units and repackaged using 23 different financing sources. It is strategically located in downtown Denver, at the junction of the 16th Street Pedestrian/Transitway Mall and the city's light-rail system, which began operation in fall 1994.

For nearly 100 years, the Denver Dry Goods department store served as the retail heart of downtown Denver, the place where generations of Denver residents shopped. But fortunes changed, and in 1987 the building was sold and the store closed.

With the beloved Denver Dry facing reincarnation as a parking lot, the Denver Urban Renewal Authority (DURA) stepped in and purchased the building in 1988. After several false starts, DURA selected the Affordable Housing Development Corporation (AHDC) as project developer and, together, DURA and AHDC resurrected the Denver Dry, fashioning it into a vibrant mixed-use project. Ultimately,

The Denver Dry Goods Building, a landmark department store structure in the heart of downtown Denver, has been reborn as a mixed-use development.

the key to the Denver Dry's resurrection was an echo of its past: just as the building was built in increments, so its reconstruction and reuse were accomplished piece by piece. The mammoth structure was broken down, figuratively and legally, into smaller development packages that were easier to manage and finance. In these smaller pieces, separate housing, retail, and office units were planned and then variously bundled together into financing and construction packages.

The adaptive use of the Denver Dry Goods Building has been successful for both the developers and the city of Denver. The two national retailers who have leased space in the project (T.J. Maxx and Media Play) are the first national large-space retailers to locate in downtown Denver in ten years. The housing component, which leased up in just two months, has had as many as 200 people on a waiting list for units. The project has been a catalyst for six other residential projects and eight other historic renovation projects in downtown Denver.

Smart Growth Characteristics

Mixed-Use and Adaptive-Use Development
The developer began by gutting the Denver Dry Goods Building's vacated retail space. Phase I of this development consisted of 51 units of affordable and market-rate housing, 73,370 square feet of retail space, and 28,780 square feet of office space. Phase II consisted of an additional 42,000 square feet of retail space. Phase III provided 77,000 square feet of residential loft space. Renovations to the building's historic elements included the removal of more than 30 layers of white, lead-based paint to expose the building's original orange-red brick, sandstone, and limestone surface, as well as the renovation of its original wood windows.

Public/Private Partnership
Organizationally, the development of Phase I was split between two limited partnerships, the Denver Building Housing, Ltd., and the Denver Dry Retail, L.P. The first partnership, the Denver Building Housing, Ltd., was responsible for the development of 51 rental apartments and office space for the Denver Metro Convention and Visitors Bureau. This partnership was made up of two entities, Fannie Mae, which purchased the tax credits and provided the equity for the deal, and the Denver Dry Development Corporation, a nonprofit 501(c)(3) corporation formed by DURA. The partnership selected AHDC as the fee developer for these portions of the project. The second Phase I partnership, the Denver Dry Retail, L.P., was responsible for development of the entire second floor of the building, consisting of the T.J. Maxx store and office space for DURA. The Denver Dry Retail Corporation, an affiliate of AHDC, is the general partner of the Denver Dry Retail, L.P.

The Phase II development team consisted of a single limited partnership, the Denver Dry Retail II, L.P., also an affiliate of AHDC. This partnership was responsible for the development of the Media Play store in the basement and the first floor of the 16th Street building.

Smart Growth Challenges

Financing and Leasing Complications
In the depressed real estate market of the late 1980s, no private buyer emerged to save the Denver Dry. As a last resort, the city and DURA stepped in and purchased the building for $6.9 million. The city financed approximately half of the purchase price, and a consortium of local banks and union pension funds financed the remainder.

Over the next two years, several developers responded to DURA's requests for proposals, offering a variety of adaptive use schemes, including a retail mall, a hotel, an aquarium, movie theaters, and upscale housing, but none was able to obtain leasing or financing commitments. These failures convinced DURA to break the building down into smaller pieces. This allowed DURA to sell two floors of the building to the Robert Waxman Camera Company, and helped make the rest of the project possible.

Infrastructure Deficits

The Denver Dry Goods Building required extensive infrastructure improvements to enable the old building to accommodate new uses. Separate, dedicated elevators for the housing and office uses were constructed from the existing department store elevator banks. New, direct access also was provided to the second-floor retail space.

Significant fire and safety improvements for the entire building were put in place simultaneously. New heating, ventilation, and air conditioning (HVAC) and electrical systems also were installed. Evaporative coolers were installed in lieu of central air conditioning in the apartments, with city steam used for heating.

Design challenges included how to use the deep bays of the existing space and how to bring light to the apartments' deep interiors. Solutions included wide hallways with adjacent leasable storage units and clerestory windows to light interior bedrooms.

Lessons Learned

⊙ While large, unconventional adaptive use projects like this one may not be feasible when viewed monolithically, breaking a project up into smaller components and packages may allow for a variety of development and financing options.

⊙ Housing can be a valuable partner in a commercial project, as it provides a 24-hour presence and stimulates an active retail environment.

⊙ A public/private partnership, such as that between DURA and AHDC, can be most successful when the approach is open on both sides and the parties work by consensus.

Project Data

Land Use Plan
(in square feet, unless otherwise noted)

Site area	1.15 acres
Gross building area	
Office	28,780
Retail	115,370
Residential	124,235
Circulation and common areas	81,615
Total	350,000

Other Data

Average annual commercial rents	
Office	$12.74 per square foot
Retail	$10 per square foot
Average monthly residential rents	$615
Average annual retail sales	$250 to $650 per square foot
Length and type of leases	
Office	Ten to 15 years full service
Retail	15 to 20 years triple net

Development Costs

Site acquisition cost	$ 6,900,000*
Construction costs	$28,592,634
Soft costs	$7,569,157
Total	$43,061,791

*Includes $900,000 for asbestos removal.

Development Schedule

Site purchased	July 1988
Planning started	July 1988
Construction started	January 1993
Sales/leasing started	July 1993
Phase I completed	October 1993
Phase II completed	May 1994
Phase III completed	August 1999

Information Contact

Denver Urban Renewal Authority
1555 California Street, Suite 200
Denver, Colorado 80202
303-295-3872

CASE STUDY: Downtown Park
Bellevue, Washington

Smart Growth Characteristics

⊙ Public/private partnership

⊙ Open space protection

⊙ Downtown revitalization

Smart Growth Challenges

⊙ Public/political opposition

⊙ Financing complications

The 20-acre Downtown Park is located in the heart of Bellevue, a suburb of Seattle.

The Project

Downtown Park is a 20-acre oasis in the heart of downtown Bellevue, a suburb ten miles east of Seattle. The design of the park was selected by a juried competition and features a large, circular, grassy meadow in its center, surrounded by a canal and a 20-foot-wide walkway lined with plane trees and obelisk-shaped light standards. The park's formal entrance is through a boulevard on the north side, which offers views of the park and the city beyond. Located at the western fringe of Bellevue's central business district and just north of historic Old Bellevue, Downtown Park is a major component of Bellevue's downtown master plan. It also provides a highly valued amenity for the people who work in nearby offices and for those who live in the area.

Under the leadership of then-mayor Cary Bozeman, the city acquired most of the site for the park (17.5 acres) from the Bellevue School District in 1983, after the school district had declared the land surplus. The remainder of the site was acquired in 1988; a few further additions have been made to it since then. (Planning continues for the southeastern portion of the park, which will complete the original design.) Controversy over the siting and the high cost of the park surrounded the acquisition of the land. Some citizens questioned the wisdom of

developing a downtown park at all. At the time, downtown Bellevue served largely
as a nine-to-five office core, but Bozeman saw the park as an investment that
would help encourage the development of higher-density housing in the area.

Financing the park became something of a roller-coaster ride. The site acquisition
was paid for with councilmanic bonds, but a 1984 general obligation bond issue to
cover the park's development failed to gather sufficient voter support. In response
to this defeat, a coalition of the city's civic and business leaders formed a nonprofit
corporation, which leased the site from the city and then raised $1.8 million to
begin developing the park. After this effort, which generated significant publicity
and support from major corporations, public support for the park grew. Voters subsequently approved bond issues to cover the park's further development costs.

The park has been successful in a number of ways. Land values in the immediate
vicinity have more than doubled, and the park has served as a catalyst for new,
higher-density residential development. Some points of debate remain, such as
how to provide sufficient parking for the park along with the rest of the downtown
area. However, by providing an attractive open space in the heart of the city, by
encouraging public and private interest in park development, and by serving as
the keystone of the city's park system, this project has demonstrated that it is possible to promote smart growth without building buildings.

Smart Growth Characteristics

Public/Private Partnership

The creation of Downtown Park would have been impossible without the unprecedented partnership between the city and the private sector. As noted above, a
coalition of citizens and businesses contributed their time, effort, and money to
create the park. This cooperation began with the sponsorship of the design competition and continued with the lease arrangement for the parkland and the mas-
sive—and successful—fundraising effort. The partnership arrangement caused
some tensions along the way, particularly over who had the authority to plan and
implement the park's design. However, the two sides learned to trust each other
and to cooperate. This model for park development has become a way of life in
the city of Bellevue.

Open Space Protection

Before Downtown Park was developed, downtown Bellevue was lacking in open
space. Moreover, if this part of downtown was to develop as the city hoped, with

a greater intensity and variety of land uses, it would need a significant open space. In the early 1980s, Mayor Bozeman realized that it would be many years before the park would achieve its potential, but that waiting any longer would allow land costs to become prohibitively high. This foresighted development now serves as a valuable place for reflection and recreation, while also enhancing downtown's pedestrian system and fostering a sense of place.

Downtown Revitalization

New residential development has begun in the area around Downtown Park. In 1994, a 97-unit condominium project—which was among the first downtown housing projects built in Bellevue in years—opened on the edge of the park and sold out almost immediately. The park, along with the other amenities that have been developed downtown (including a regional library and new retail stores), has strongly encouraged the development of hundreds of additional residential units in the surrounding area. As one residential developer has said, a site next to Downtown Park is "a blue-ribbon location."

Smart Growth Challenges

Public/Political Opposition

Early on, not everyone in Bellevue was convinced that this site should serve as a park. Some thought the site was inappropriate for a "central" park; others felt that the cost was too high and that the voters should have had a say in approving the bonds that paid for the land acquisition. The leadership of both the city government and the business community, however, brought people around to the cause. Moreover, phasing the development of the park helped to demonstrate the benefits that it would provide. Since this project began, park development has become very popular in Bellevue, with the results from Downtown Park spurring additional investments in other parks around the city.

Financing Complications

Putting together the financing for Downtown Park was no easy matter. Indeed, the initial public resistance to spending the money needed to develop the park forced the city's leaders to search for novel solutions. Part of the reason the fundraising campaign was so successful was the creation of a private entity to develop the park; many contributors believed that this group would manage the funds, and the park's creation, more efficiently than would the city government. The professional marketing efforts that supported the fundraising campaign generated very positive results, but would have been impossible for the city to undertake alone. By combining the strengths of the public and private sectors, the coalition raised enough money to make Downtown Park a reality.

Lessons Learned

⊙ The public/private model used to develop Downtown Park has proven very effective, and is now a commonly used technique in the provision of open space in the city of Bellevue. Such partnerships can be difficult to manage, however. Both sides need to have confidence in one another and must be willing to compromise.

⊙ Creating parks and open space can be an effective technique to promote development, as well as livability, in the surrounding area by providing a highly valued community amenity.

⊙ One successful park project can foster political support for the development or acquisition of additional parks and open space. Downtown Park has helped tremendously in the creation of a network of parks in Bellevue.

Project Data

Development Costs

Site acquisition	$23,618,000
Site improvement	$5,302,733
Construction (buildings)	$385,600
Soft costs	$1,062,245
Total	$30,368,578

Financing

Funding Source	Amount	Percent of Total
Private	$1,766,000	6%
Local	$28,234,000	94%
Total	$30,000,000	100%

Development Schedule

Initial site acquired	December 1983
Planning started	August 1983
Design competition conducted	July 1984
Master plan approved	April 1985
Construction started (Phase I)	August 1986
Construction completed (Phase I)	September 1987
Construction started (Phase II)	September 1989
Construction completed (Phase II)	September 1990
Park opened (Phase II)	September 1990

Information Contact

City of Bellevue
Department of Parks and Community Services
P.O. Box 90012
Bellevue, Washington 98009
425-452-6881
www.ci.bellevue.wa.us

CASE STUDY: **East Lake Commons**
Decatur, Georgia

Smart Growth Characteristics

⊙ Conservation design

⊙ Collaborative planning

⊙ Traditional neighborhood design

Smart Growth Challenges

⊙ Regulatory barriers

⊙ Financing complications

**The 67 market-rate townhomes in East Lake
Commons are clustered to create a sense of
community and to preserve public spaces,
which include a four-acre organic garden.**

The Project

By blending affordability, ecology, and community, the developers of East Lake
Commons have transformed an abandoned lot into a vibrant urban residential
community. Located just five miles from downtown Atlanta, East Lake Commons
is a market-rate infill development. The project consists of 67 fee-simple, market-
rate homes that range from a 1,210-square-foot flat to a 1,948-square-foot, four-
bedroom, single-family house; a 5,400-square-foot community building; and a
four-acre community farm. Half of the 20-acre site is preserved as garden and
open space. The project successfully blends many of the innovative concepts of
collaborative housing with elements of traditional community development.

To jump start the project, developer Jack Morse began to work with a group of 17
households that had been looking for a site for the development of a cohousing
community. (Cohousing is a form of collaborative housing that is characterized by
privately owned homes supported by a community building that typically includes
a kitchen, play areas, and meeting rooms. Cohousing communities aim to allow
homeowners to enjoy the benefits of homeownership while also taking advantage
of shared community services and amenities.) By forging an agreement with this

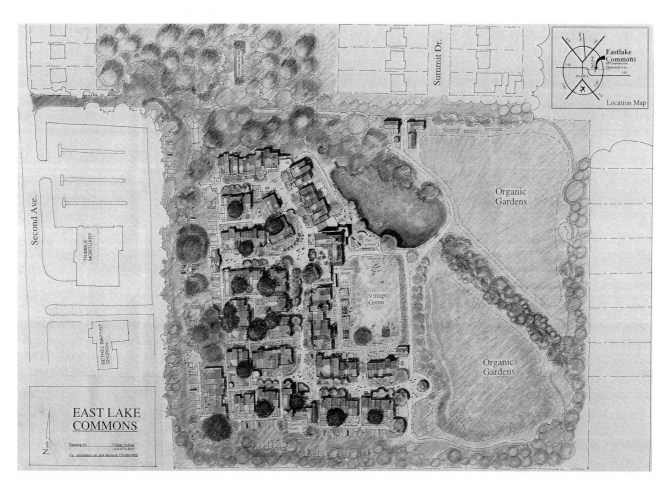

Summit Dr.

Eastlake Commons
Location Map

Organic Gardens

Second Ave.

TRIMBLE MORTUARY

Playground

Common House

Village Green

Organic Gardens

BETHEL BAPTIST CHURCH

Common House

EAST LAKE COMMONS

Planning by: Village Habitat
                    (404) 876-8001
For information call Jack Morse at 770-908-0855

N

East Lake Commons's site plan was designed to create a pedestrian-oriented village cluster.

cohousing group, the developer was able to streamline the predevelopment process by essentially preselling 17 units. This gave the project the critical mass necessary to move forward.

The East Lake Commons site plan features a pedestrian-oriented village cluster consisting of community spaces, semiprivate courtyards, and groups of private homes. Pedestrian lanes connect the spaces within the community and vary in size to convey the progression from public to private spaces. Sitting areas are dispersed along the pedestrian lanes to maximize pedestrian interaction.

The project's architecture combines elements from the area's urban and agricultural heritage. Each colorful home features a gracious front porch, creating a welcoming residential streetscape. The community building (Common House), designed to be the centerpiece of East Lake Commons, contains a kitchen and a dining area as well as facilities for guests, recreation, and education.

The site plan keeps automobiles outside the village cluster by grouping parking areas along the perimeter of the site. (The longest distance from a parking area to a home is less than the length of the average supermarket parking lot.) Stalls holding large carts are spaced around the parking areas for the residents' convenience.

Smart Growth Characteristics

Conservation Design

The high-density clustered site plan allowed for the preservation of approximately 55 percent of the site as green space that is used for a community farm, stream buffers, and woodland areas. The farm, which is owned by East Lake Commons residents and leased to a local farmer free of charge, provides a unique open space resource in this urban setting. (Residents and neighbors who participate in a farmshare program pay the farmer $360 per year for a 30-week supply of organic produce.) The project's environmentally responsible design dramatically enhanced the marketability of this infill site.

Collaborative Planning

Early in the development process, the developer met with local civic leaders, who voiced a desire for market-rate, for-sale housing that targeted working professionals seeking an urban alternative to suburban living. Morse soon recognized that there was pent-up demand in the Atlanta metropolitan area for a residential development that offered community-based amenities within an urban context, and accordingly repositioned his predevelopment efforts to target this market.

In addition to working with local civic leaders to determine what type of project the community wanted, Morse also collaborated with the original 17-household cohousing group to identify an appropriate architectural style for the project. Under his guidance, the cohousing group worked with Chuck Durrett (an Atlanta-based cohousing consultant) to develop architectural themes and floor plans for the project's housing units and community building. Involving these future residents in building design helped the developer to better forecast market preferences.

Traditional Neighborhood Design

While collaborative or cohousing can increase a developer's scope of work considerably, it also offers significant benefits, including product differentiation, increased absorption, and enhanced marketability.

Most of the project's residents have chosen the community because of its convenient urban setting and for the intentional community offered by the cohousing program, through which residents organize committees that collectively manage the community's affairs. Meals are prepared by community volunteers several times each week at the Common House, and the community holds bimonthly general business meetings and has established a Web site that posts community news and information about upcoming events. A listserve e-mail system also is used to contact residents on a regular basis.

Smart Growth Challenges

Regulatory Barriers

As with most high-density, pedestrian-oriented site plans, special considerations were required during the permitting and approval process. The developer was required to rezone the property to allow for the construction of 67 fee-simple townhomes under a planned unit development (PUD) designation. Once approved as a PUD, the project was granted increased flexibility with regard to numerous zoning standards, including setbacks, minimum lot sizes, and parking requirements. To meet municipal fire codes, many of the project's pedestrian lanes were built to allow firetruck access. This eliminated the need to install sprinklers, dramatically decreasing construction costs and increasing the project's affordability.

Financing Complications

The project's inventive design required the developer to be equally inventive when it came to financing. Morse strategically leveraged grant money and soft money, as well as his equity in the land, to creatively finance the project's predevelopment soft costs as well as the construction of residential units, the community building, and the farm.

By forming a strategic alliance with the Atlanta Resource Foundation, Morse was able to secure more than $300,000 in grant money for the construction and operation of the Common House and the farm, which also are used as an environmental education site for inner-city youth and other neighbors. In addition, each homebuyer contributes $5,000 out of closing proceeds for the design and development of the Common House.

The Cousins Family Foundation provided a $200,000, interest-free loan to cover upfront soft costs. Morse used these funds, coupled with the land, as equity to secure nonrecourse construction financing. The construction lender, Sun Trust Bank–Atlanta, required the developer to secure firm contracts on 25 units prior to construction. Given Morse's relationship with the cohousing group, this was readily achievable.

Lessons Learned

⊙ Working with an existing group of 17 households that were interested in establishing a collaborative/cohousing community enabled the developer to quickly generate the critical mass necessary to initiate the redevelopment of an underused urban infill site.

⊙ The consensus decision-making nature of collaborative/cohousing communities can slow the development process considerably. The developer of East Lake Commons, however, acted independently during the site planning and permitting process, allowing for the timely delivery of an entitled site to the market.

⊙ A "one-size-fits-all" approach does not work in sustainable or environmentally responsible development. All development decisions must be site specific. For example, the decision to decrease the project's impervious surfaces by using gravel, rather than hardscape, on pedestrian pathways lead to poor results.

⊙ Developers should take advantage of the skills, talents, and enthusiasm of community residents. Numerous East Lake Commons homeowners—including a computer programmer who created the Web site—helped make the project work.

Project Data

Land Uses

Site area	20 acres
Total dwelling units	
Planned	67
Completed	30
	(58 under contract)
Gross density	3.35 units per acre

Land Use Plan

Use	Acres
Detached residential	.25
Attached/multifamily residential	7.5
Roads	2.25
Common open space	6
Organic farm	4
Total	20

Dwelling Unit Data

Unit Type	Unit Size (in square feet)	Number Planned/Built	Sales Prices
Two-bedroom "A"	1,235	13/9	$115,750–$120,000
Two-bedroom	1,417	23/11	$135,750–$160,000
Two-bedroom "flat"	1,210	3/3	$109,000–$125,000
Three-bedroom	1,740	27/10	$155,750–$210,000
Four-bedroom	1,948	1/1	$240,000

Development Costs (Projected)

Site acquisition cost	$356,000
Site improvement costs	$1,336,680
Construction cost	$6,322,208
Soft costs	$1,677,379
Total at buildout	$9,692,267

Development Schedule

Site purchased	February 1996
Planning started	March 1996
Construction started	May 1998
Sales started	November 1997
First closing	April 1999
Phase I completed	May 2000
Project completed	September 2000

Information Contact

East Lake Commons, Inc.
1836 Second Ave
Decatur, Georgia 30032
404-784-1122

CASE STUDY: MCI Center
Washington, D.C.

The MCI Center, which has spurred redevelopment in downtown Washington, D.C., seats 20,600 spectators for events and includes retail space and a restaurant.

Smart Growth Characteristics

⊙ Downtown revitalization

⊙ Public/private partnership

⊙ Transit- and pedestrian-oriented design

Smart Growth Challenges

⊙ Site constraints

⊙ Regulatory barriers

The Project

The MCI Center is a multipurpose sports and entertainment facility located in the Gallery Place redevelopment area in northwest Washington, D.C. The center is home to three professional sports teams: the National Hockey League's Washington Capitals, the National Basketball Association's Washington Wizards, and the Women's National Basketball Association's Washington Mystics. The arena, which seats approximately 20,600 spectators, also is used for amateur sporting events, concerts and shows, and other social events. Retail space and a restaurant within the building complement the arena, and proximity to the Metrorail mass transit system eases parking requirements and provides convenient access for spectators.

The project symbolizes a renewed commitment to downtown Washington. MCI Center developer and Capitals and Wizards owner Abe Pollin had moved his teams and arena from the inner city to a suburban site in the 1970s. Amongst the turbulent economic and social problems plaguing downtown Washington in the mid-1990s, however, Pollin recommitted to the urban core by partnering with the District of Columbia to build a new arena and bring his teams back to the city center.

The success of the project for both Pollin and the District demonstrates that overcoming some of the more typical urban redevelopment challenges—such as land acquisition problems, site constraints, environmental contamination, and legislative hurdles—can be a profitable endeavor.

The MCI Center's success also can be measured by new revitalization efforts in the neighborhood. Restaurants, hotels, and a new convention center are providing a wave of revitalization in the surrounding blocks. The MCI Center is one of the catalysts for this revitalization and is helping to remake the District's image from the inside out.

Smart Growth Characteristics

Downtown Revitalization
The District's Redevelopment Land Agency (RLA) assembled the site occupied by the MCI Center. To satisfy site requirements, the city purchased a parcel of land that was adjacent to a parcel that it already owned. This previously owned site contained soil contamination that had to be cleaned up, while the newly acquired land held old government office buildings that had to be demolished. The MCI Center has filled an unused, unattractive urban space and has served as a catalyst for revitalization efforts in surrounding neighborhoods.

The center is home to three professional sports teams: the National Hockey League's Washington Capitals, the National Basketball Association's Washington Wizards, and the Women's National Basketball Association's Washington Mystics.

Public/Private Partnership

The District of Columbia agreed to manage the process and become financially responsible for acquiring and assembling the land, demolishing existing structures, and remediating all contamination. Pollin's team financed and managed the construction of the arena. Complications with public financing, private developer deadlines, and unforeseen soil contaminants made the partnership's efficiency and effectiveness crucial to the project's success.

Transit- and Pedestrian-Oriented Design

The District of Columbia constructed a new pedestrian connection from the arena to a Washington Metrorail station. An estimated 60 to 65 percent of all ticket holders for sports events take public transit to and from the arena.

Smart Growth Challenges

Site Constraints

Soil contamination from years of commercial laundry operations and from the more than 20 heating oil and fuel storage tanks found underground plagued a portion of the site. The District's commitment to cleaning up this contamination ultimately proved critical to the project's success, as remediation costs soared above initial estimates.

Regulatory Barriers

Pollin was able to get a land lease from the District of Columbia through the RLA. At the beginning of the development process, however, pending legislative actions made the District unable to issue the necessary tax-exempt bonds to finance the project. The District took a bank loan on the understanding that if the requisite legislation were enacted, the RLA would issue tax-exempt revenue bonds to refinance the bank loan. The legislation eventually passed, and the tax-exempt bonds were issued.

Lessons Learned

⊙ At the time that Abe Pollin joined forces with the District, the city was known for its overwhelming and unworkable bureaucracy. This made it imperative to establish a coordinated project task force and put in place a decision-making framework with clear lines of authority.

⊙ In the case of a brownfield redevelopment project such as the MCI Center, thorough and accurate site assessment is critical to keep the project on budget. The city ultimately spent over five times the initial estimated cost for environmental remediation.

⊙ The city's streamlining of the development review process allowed Pollin's development team to proceed quickly.

Project Data

Land Uses

Site area	5.2 acres
Gross building area (GBA)	1,050,000 square feet
Arena area	715,000 square feet
Retail space	85,000 square feet
Parking	250,000 square feet
	(550 spaces)

Development Costs

Developer's costs	
Construction costs	$260 million
Soft costs	$40 million
Total	$300 million
Public funds	
Site preparation	$51.54 million
Other	$13.98 million
Total	$65.52 million
Total costs	$365.52 million

Development Schedule

Planning started	1995
Land leased from RLA	July 17, 1995
Construction started	October 18, 1995
Construction completed	December 2, 1997

Information Contacts

John Stranix
President, MCI Center
Washington Sports & Entertainment
601 F Street, N.W.
Washington, D.C. 20004
202-628-3200

Jose Nunez
Washington, D.C., Department of Housing and Community Development,
    Development and Finance Division
801 North Capitol Street, N.E., Second Floor
Washington, D.C. 20002
202-442-7288

CASE STUDY: The Can Company
Baltimore, Maryland

Smart Growth Characteristics

⊙ Adaptive use/historic preservation

⊙ Public/private partnership

⊙ Collaborative planning

Smart Growth Challenges

⊙ Parking limitations

⊙ Financing complications

The Can Company is a mixed-use development that is serving as the linchpin to the revitalization of Canton, an older Baltimore neighborhood

The Project

The Can Company is an adaptive use project on the site of the former American Can Company factory in Baltimore's Canton neighborhood. The mixed-use development includes more than 60,000 square feet of retail and 140,000 square feet of office space and serves as the centerpiece of southeast Baltimore's renaissance. It is located on a recently upgraded thoroughfare, Boston Street, and looks out on the Baltimore waterfront. A total of 290 cars can be accommodated in a surface parking lot and a garage constructed within one of the existing buildings; a lease agreement with an adjacent supermarket adds another 30 spaces. The Can Company rests between the old Canton neighborhood—with its blocks of established housing and corner bars and markets—and the new Canton neighborhood, which features waterfront condominiums, townhomes, and marinas. It has successfully blended the new with the old through architectural design, tenant recruitment, and community involvement.

In 1895, the Norton Tin Can and Plate Company, which later became the American Can Company, constructed its first building on the 9.5-acre site. The American Can Company continued to prosper through most of the century until the factory

DAP Products, Inc., moved its world headquarters to the Can Company in 1998.

closed in the late 1980s. The vacant buildings blighted the Canton community until 1994, when Safeway purchased 5.2 acres of the site, demolished some existing buildings, and built a 50,000-square-foot supermarket. In 1997, Struever Bros., Eccles & Rouse, a local mid-sized development and construction company, purchased the remaining 4.3 acres, which included 300,000 square feet of the most historically significant buildings on the site. Soon after the purchase, Struever Bros. began developing the Can Company.

During the initial development phase, a portion of the site was identified as contaminated, as a result of poor disposal of lead solder from the existing soldering plant. Struever Bros. addressed the issue by taking advantage of the Brownfields Voluntary Cleanup and Revitalization Program (a component of Maryland's smart growth initiative), which gives participants limited relief from liability for past contamination. (Before the state offered such programs, concerns regarding brownfield liability could have deterred the redevelopment of the American Can site.) Struever Bros. has met Maryland Department of Environment cleanup requirements, and was the first property owner in the state to successfully complete this smart growth program.

Consisting of the four-story Signature Building, the three-story Factory Building, the two-story 1895 Building, the boiler house, and a small annex, the Can Company is a highly integrated mixed-use complex. In September 1997, DAP Products, Inc.—the world's largest manufacturer of sealants and adhesives—signed the first lease at the Can Company, and the 1895 Building was developed on a fast-track schedule to allow the company, the project's largest tenant, to move its world headquarters to Baltimore by March 1998. DAP Products employs 125 people and serves as the Can Company's commercial anchor tenant.

In hopes of attracting young high-tech companies to Baltimore, the Baltimore Development Corporation, the Maryland Economic Development Corporation, and the federal government teamed up to create the Emerging Technology Center, a high-tech incubator. The center's 48,000 square feet of office space take up the entire third floor of the Factory Building and will accommodate up to 30 start-up companies. The Signature Building is home to Bibelot Books and Music, Donna's Coffee Bar, and gr8, an Internet marketing firm. Can Company tenants have preserved the complex's industrial features, which include brick facades, high ceilings, and expansive windows, while adding modern features to create unique spaces that take advantage of the site's historic character.

The developer of the Can Company included an extensive community involvement process that was seen as critical to the success of the project.

In just over a year, the Can Company's office space was 100 percent leased and all but 2,000 square feet of its retail space was leased. The project has established an employment, retail, and entertainment hub in the community. It has created approximately 650 jobs, almost equaling the 800 jobs the American Can Company generated in its heyday. Demand for housing in the Canton neighborhood has increased exponentially. Between 1996 and 2000, housing prices increased 40 percent, average time on the market was cut nearly in half, the percentage of homeowners in the neighborhood increased, and reinvestment took place in the existing housing stock near the Can Company. Bill Struever, president of Struever Bros., Eccles & Rouse, summarizes the success of the project by stating, "If we had ten American Cans, we could fill them us as fast as we could build them."

Smart Growth Characteristics

Adaptive Use/Historic Preservation

Protecting and restoring the existing buildings was central to the development philosophy employed by Struever Bros. Complying with U.S. Department of the Interior redevelopment guidelines, Struever Bros. restored steel-sash windows, reglazed 15,000 panes of glass using DAP glazing, repaired and repointed brick walls, constructed new corrugated metal and built-up roofs for all five buildings, and salvaged the factory's distinctive stacks and ventilators. Struever Bros. embraced most of these adaptations because it recognized that the preservation of historic features was central to the type of complex it sought to develop.

Public/Private Partnership

The public sector's role in the project was substantial, and helped to secure its early successes. In addition to the support received through Maryland's brownfields program, the project qualified for a ten-year property tax abatement through Baltimore's property tax credit program for the rehabilitation of historic structures. This also allowed it to receive historic tax credits and other state funds. Vital infrastructure improvements, particularly road improvements to Boston Street, helped attract tenants.

Collaborative Planning

Working with neighborhood residents was central to the Struever Bros. approach. From the outset, citizen involvement in the design of the Can Company helped to facilitate its rapid development and to secure the permits for the Can Company's bars and restaurants. Struever Bros. worked with the community to ensure that its

The Can Company's interior is characterized by high ceilings, expansive windows, and various modern decors that create unique spaces.

concerns and interests regarding the redevelopment of the site were addressed. Preserving the buildings and maintaining the character of the community was important to neighborhood residents, who in the past had rejected development proposals for the site that included razing its structures.

Smart Growth Challenges

Parking Limitations

Providing adequate parking can be difficult for any infill development or redevelopment project. The Can Company's developer addressed this issue by adapting the first and second floors of the Factory Building into a 170-space parking garage. During the day, the lot is available only to employees of the project's commercial tenants. In the evening, however, the garage is open, free of charge, to any patron of the Can Company's retailers. While the only other on-site parking consists of a 120-space surface parking lot, the Can Company also leases 30 parking spaces from the Safeway supermarket, and has secured 45 parking spots for tenants of the Emerging Technology Center in a public lot located on Boston Street. The Can Company is not accessible by either light-rail or subway lines.

Financing Complications

Financing a complicated adaptive use project in the heart of Baltimore was a difficult undertaking. A number of creative traditional and nontraditional financing techniques enabled the developer to obtain the resources necessary to complete the Can Company. Financing included an equity contribution from the developer, a bridge loan for land purchase and initial construction, a construction and permanent loan from Riggs Bank, the purchase of historic tax credits from the Bank of America (through syndication by the Enterprise Social Investment Corporation), and an equity investment by Fannie Mae's American Communities Fund.

Lessons Learned

⊙ Community involvement in the design of the project was crucial. Katherine Hearn, project director, Struever Bros., notes that "the community's involvement must come early and continue throughout the process. If [citizens] are surprised with how it is progressing, the project could be severely sidetracked." Struever Bros. has continued its commitment to community participation by partnering with Canton Middle School to teach students how to develop properties through a course that includes drawing to scale, architectural design, and statistics.

⊙ Developers must be persistent when working with multiple public agencies, whose support can help to move a project forward and resolve unexpected problems. Local and state agencies, helped Struever Bros. solve the problems that arose when the developer discovered that a portion of the Can Company site was contaminated.

⊙ The Can Company illustrates that the public and private sectors can work together to produce a high-quality development that both serves the public interest and is profitable for the developer. The project also demonstrates that incentives provided through Maryland's Smart Growth Program and by the city of Baltimore can help facilitate urban renewal.

Project Data

Land Uses (in square feet, unless otherwise noted)

Site area	4.3 acres
On-site parking	290 spaces
Off-street parking	45 spaces
Gross building area (GBA)	
Office	140,000
Retail	60,000
Parking	100,000
Total	300,000

Land Use Plan

Use	Acres	Percent of Site
Buildings	3.3	76%
Streets/surface parking	8	19%
Landscaping/open space	2	5%
Total	4.3	100%

Other Data

Office

Occupancy rate	100%
Number of tenants	11
Average tenant size	12,727 square feet
Annual rents	Approximately $15 to $20 per square foot
Average lease length	Five to 15 years
Typical lease terms	Full service; one parking space per 1,000 square feet of leasable space

Retail

Occupancy rate	85%
Annual rents	Approximately $15 to $30 per square foot
Average annual sales	Approximately $200 per square foot
Average lease length	Five to 15 years

Development Costs

Site acquisition costs	$972,500
Site improvement costs	$1,000,000
Construction costs	$18,300,000
Soft costs	$7,397,000
Total	$27,669,500

Development Schedule

Site purchased	August 1997
Planning started	June 1996
Construction started	September 1997
Sales/leasing started	September 1996
Project completed	December 1998

Information Contact

Struever Bros., Eccles & Rouse, Inc.
519 North Charles Street
Baltimore, Maryland 21201
410-332-1352

CASE STUDY: Pearl Court Apartments
Portland, Oregon

Smart Growth Characteristics

⊙ Affordable housing

⊙ Public/private partnership

⊙ Environmental features

⊙ Transit-oriented design

Smart Growth Challenges

⊙ Financing complications

⊙ Parking limitations

The 199 units at Pearl Court Apartments are rented at rates that are affordable to low- and moderate-income households.

The Project

Pearl Court Apartments, completed in September 1997, is a full-block development at the edge of downtown Portland in the city's emerging River District, a new neighborhood growing out of 70 acres of vacant railyard between downtown and the Willamette River. The building's 199 apartments are rented at rates that are affordable to low- and moderate-income households. The building features a library; a formal, two-level lobby with a fireplace; numerous lounges and outdoor decks; and a large bicycle room. The apartments surround a landscaped courtyard.

Built at a density of more than 211 units per acre, Pearl Court exceeds the density of any project built in the area to date, as well as that of most projects in Portland. It thus furthers one of the main goals of the city's River District plan—to stem sprawling development in the metropolitan area and capture growth in the central city by locating housing close to employment, retail, and services. In addition, the site's proximity to downtown, the transit mall (which provides free bus service in the central city area), the light-rail line, and a future streetcar line allowed the developer to build at a very low parking ratio—18 spaces for 199 apartments.

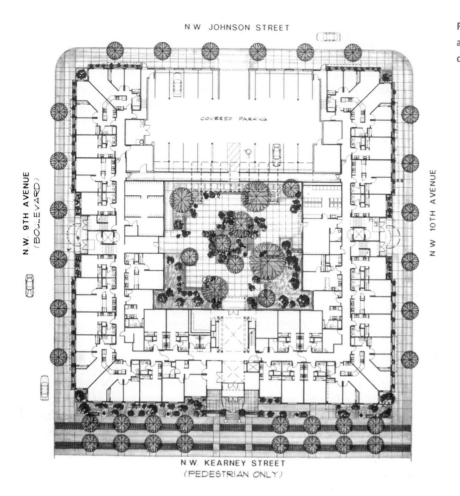

NW JOHNSON STREET

COVERED PARKING

N.W. 9TH AVENUE (BOULEVARD)

N.W. 10TH AVENUE

N.W. KEARNEY STREET
(PEDESTRIAN ONLY)

Pearl Court's apartments, library, lounges, and bicycle room surround a landscaped courtyard.

The Pearl Court site—next to a viaduct ramp and the city's main post office parking lot—made it more suitable for rental than for-sale housing. Moreover, the developer viewed Pearl Court as an opportunity to realize one of the central goals of the River District plan—to create a mixed-income neighborhood.

Pearl Court was part of a large brownfield site; its soil was contaminated by railroad operations and its groundwater by an old manufactured gas plant nearby. Burlington Northern Railroad had been working with the Oregon Department of Environmental Quality (DEQ) on a risk and feasibility assessment of the entire 40-acre railyard area. When Prendergast & Associates began assembling the site for Pearl Court, the developer asked Burlington Northern and DEQ to accelerate the assessment and remediation of the one-acre parcel. Although both parties were concerned about setting a precedent, they agreed to the cleanup program.

Burlington Northern quickly cleaned up the soil, and DEQ agreed to issue a prospective purchaser agreement (PPA) to remove any liability from the Housing Authority of Portland (HAP, a partner in the project), the partnership, lenders, or investors for any existing conditions. This was the first time that a PPA was used in conjunction with a Section 42 low-income housing tax credit (LIHTC) project.

Despite the complexity of an undertaking involving brownfield cleanup, intricate financing, and myriad public/private partnerships, Pearl Court was on a fast-track development/construction schedule. Although many tax-credit projects entail two to three years of planning before construction starts, the developer closed on the financing one year after planning began and completed construction less than a year after that. From the start, the architect, developer, and contractor worked together as a team, which helped the project stay on schedule and on budget.

Smart Growth Characteristics

Affordable Housing

Unlike many affordable housing developments, Pearl Court was begun by a private developer. The 199-unit apartment building, a joint venture of Prendergast & Associates and HAP, offers studio and one- and two-bedroom apartments to residents earning between 40 percent and 60 percent of the area median income. The building's exceptional design sets the standard for future affordable housing developments in the neighborhood and proves that high-quality affordable housing can be developed without large public subsidies.

Public/Private Partnership

The city of Portland had been studying the redevelopment potential of the River District since the early 1980s and had acquired about 30 acres on its fringe—including the passenger train station—in the late 1980s. Planning began in earnest in 1990, when local developer Pat Prendergast purchased 40 acres from Burlington Northern Railroad. A committee of civic leaders, property owners, citizen activists, and city officials convened in 1991 to develop a vision for the district. Whereas earlier plans treated the area as an extension of downtown, the committee recommended building a new medium-density residential neighborhood as part of Portland's strategy to contain urban sprawl and use existing infrastructure more effectively.

In 1995, Portland's city council adopted an ambitious vision plan for the River District. This plan called for the creation of 5,000 or more housing units to accommodate residents of all incomes in a pedestrian- and transit-oriented neighborhood connected to downtown and the river and served by a mix of retail uses, new parks, and a new streetcar line.

Prendergast knew that HAP wanted to ensure a supply of affordable housing in the River District, so he offered to sell the city the Pearl Court parcel and to develop it. HAP made an attractive development partner because of its ability to issue low-cost, tax-exempt bonds quickly and because it would be a responsible long-term owner. The developer, in turn, brought the land, development expertise, and working capital to the project.

A limited partnership was set up with HAP as the general partner. The developer eventually sold the tax credits to Fannie Mae, making it the sole limited partner of Pearl Court Limited Partnership. Prendergast & Associates assumed full development responsibilities, and HAP assumed responsibility for management after completion.

Environmental Features

The developers were committed to making Pearl Court as environmentally sustainable as the budget permitted. They worked with the local utility company, Enron Portland General Electric (PGE), which provided an environmental consultant and a comprehensive set of guidelines for constructing an "Earth Smart" building that recommended recycling construction site materials, using nontoxic (or low-toxic) paint and other materials, installing a continuous ventilation system, using recycled-content materials, providing for tenant recycling by placing a large recycling room on each floor, and installing an innovative stormwater system that recharges part of the roof runoff back into the ground rather than into the public storm sewer system.

Transit-Oriented Design

Pearl Court has access to a broad range of public and private transit services within a five-block area. These include local and long-distance buses, light-rail trains, and a future streetcar line. A main aim of the River District plan was to locate housing close to employment, retail, services, and entertainment as a way of encouraging walking, biking, and transit use. Pearl Court features a bicycle room with 72 bicycle racks, each of which can hold two bicycles. Proximity to downtown and excellent access to public transportation made it possible to include remarkably few parking spaces.

Smart Growth Challenges

Financing Complications

Compared with most other Portland public housing projects, Pearl Court represents a conservative investment of public funds. The project was financed with tax-exempt bonds, equity from the sale of 4 percent low-income housing tax credits (LIHTCs) to Fannie Mae, and a subordinate loan from the Portland Development Commission (PDC), the city's urban renewal agency. The developer worked with the city to use its resources in new ways, including bridge financing, a letter of credit, funding of construction draws, and a dept reserve guarantee.

Parking Limitations

The developers started with a parking ratio of 1:6, but when they began to explore the possibility of increasing the project size from 170 to 199 units, they found that there was no room for additional parking to serve the extra units. They solved this problem by building the additional units as low-income rentals without parking.

Lessons Learned

⊙ Pearl Court demonstrates that low-income housing can be attractive and blend well with adjacent high-end development.

⊙ The costs of including numerous environmentally sustainable and energy-conserving features are just as, if not more, appropriate for affordable housing as for market-rate projects. Following the local utility company's "Earth Smart" standards resulted in features that lower residents' heating and lighting expenses.

⊙ In hindsight, Prendergast says he would have started earlier and allotted more time to incorporate environmental features.

⊙ It is important to take a long-term perspective with a development located in an emerging neighborhood. Otherwise, it is easy to be discouraged by temporary conditions and build a lower-quality development. The lesson is to focus on what you want to build and to build it, rather than becoming distracted by existing conditions that are likely to improve in the future.

⊙ One of the keys to developing affordable housing at greater densities is to limit the amount of space devoted to parking.

⊙ Low-income housing can be well designed, with attractive, high-quality amenities, at a relatively low cost and without large subsidies. Whereas most Portland tax-credit projects require loans of $20,000 or more per unit from the city's urban renewal agency, Pearl Court borrowed only $7,000 per unit.

Project Data

Land Uses

Site area	0.94 acres
Total units	199
Gross density	211 units per acre
Off-street parking	18 spaces
Gross leasable area (GLA) occupied	98%
Monthly rents	$308–$595

Land Use Plan

Use	Acres	Percent of Site
Buildings	.72	77%
Roads/paved areas	.02	2%
Common open space	.20	21%
Total	.94	100%

Development Costs

Site acquisition costs	$750,000
Site improvement costs	$610,721
Construction costs	$7,994,044
Soft costs	$2,859,243
Total	$12,214,008
Development cost/unit	$61,377.00
Construction cost/square foot	$61.65

Development Schedule

Site purchased	1990
Planning started	October 1995
Construction started	October 1996
Leasing started	August 1997
Construction completed	September 1997
Project leased up	January 1998
	(100% occupied)

Information Contact

Prendergast & Associates
333 SW Fifth Avenue, Suite 200
Portland, Oregon 97204
503-223-6605

CASE STUDY: Washington's Landing
Pittsburgh, Pennsylvania

Smart Growth Characteristics

⊙ Public/private partnership

⊙ Mixed-use development

⊙ Open space protection

Smart Growth Challenge

⊙ Infrastructure deficits

⊙ Site constraints

The riverfront trail that runs through Washington's Landing accentuates the island's natural attributes.

The Project

Washington's Landing is a mixed-use development located on 42-acre Herr's Island, which sits on the western bank of the Allegheny River, approximately two miles from Pittsburgh's Golden Triangle. From the turn of the century until the late 1960s, the island's primary users were the Union Stock Yards and the Pittsburgh Provision and Packing Company, the city's primary meatpacking facility. By the mid 1970s, a salvage yard and a rendering plant were the only active operations on an island filled with blighted buildings, deficient infrastructure and access, and industrial debris.

The Washington's Landing project involves the revitalization of this island into a high-quality, mixed-use development encompassing a full-service marina, market-rate housing, office/research and development/light industrial uses, a rowing center, and a public park. The project was undertaken pursuant to a redevelopment plan adopted by Pittsburgh's city council in October 1983. The plan regulates development to accentuate the island's natural assets, including the waterfront areas and the secluded views of the downtown skyline. Each development parcel is situated and designed to best take advantage of these assets. A network of riverfront trails connects the public open spaces and other park facilities, and

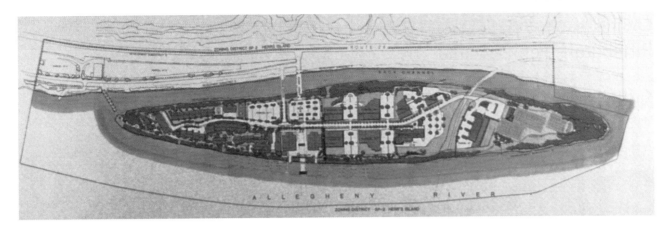

Careful planning and public/private development efforts have transformed the 42-acre Herr's Island into a mixed-use development.

pedestrian circulation is encouraged through attractive streetscaping and access to the water at entrances located at building sites.

Smart Growth Characteristics

Public/Private Partnership

The Urban Redevelopment Authority of Pittsburgh (URA) acted as land developer and prepared sites to make them competitive and to stimulate the interest of private developers. For the most part, URA eschewed the request for proposals (RFP) process in favor of attracting private developers through various financial incentives and the site's natural attributes. The significant amount of public funding involved in the redevelopment, along with financing assistance from URA and a property tax abatement program, allows office developers to offer tenants lease rates lower than those for typical downtown offices.

Mixed-Use Development

In the early 1980s, the city of Pittsburgh rezoned Herr's Island from industrial to "specially planned district" (SPD). The SPD zoning allowed for the orderly, planned development of a mixed-use project like Washington's Landing.

Open Space Protection

Five acres of riverfront trails and the public park offer residents waterfront access and recreational opportunities. The trail is connected to the main shoreline and the Three Rivers Heritage Trail by a historically rehabilitated pedestrian bridge.

Smart Growth Challenges

Infrastructure Deficits

By 1981, federal funding for infrastructure was significantly curtailed and proposed access and transportation improvements had to be revised. Only a single bridge would provide vehicle access to the island, constraining redevelopment plans, particularly for uses that generate peak-hour traffic. The following year, an assessment of the highest and best use of the site noted the island's unique features—waterfront access, seclusion, and views of the downtown skyline. The study proposed that, in addition to earlier recommendations for commercial and light industrial uses and in consideration of limited access, housing also should be developed on the island.

Site Constraints

Construction of offices began in 1987, but was halted shortly thereafter by the discovery of previously undetected soil contaminants. A consent order issued earlier from the U.S. Environmental Protection Agency (EPA) protected developers from liability for previously deposited contaminants. The developer spent the next

18 months and $3.4 million encapsulating the waste. In 1991, construction resumed and the buildings were completed in 1992 and 1993.

Lessons Learned

⊙ While no specific parking ratios were required, URA felt that requiring that buildings cover no more than 60 percent of their site would help provide adequate parking. Shared parking by office and recreational uses has further benefitted parking on the island.

⊙ Disposal of land parcels in roughly equal increments (two to four acres) has been beneficial in maintaining the orderly and well-planned development of the island and ensures that no single user dominates the site.

⊙ Partnering with selected private developers—as opposed to using the RFP process—has reduced conflicts between URA and developers. Most development on the island has been in partnership with private developers.

Project Data

Land Uses

Site area	42 acres
Marina	150 wet slips, 150 storage slips for boats
Residential	90 units
Office/research/light industrial	225,000 square feet
Rowing center	15,000 square feet
Public park and trails	5 acres
Gross leasable area (GLA) occupied	
Office, R&D, and manufacturing	90% sold or leased
Residential	80 of 90 units completed and sold
Average sales/lease prices	
Residential	$145,000–$500,000 per unit
Commercial	$9.00 to $12.00 per square foot

Development Schedule

Site purchased	1978–1981
Planning started	1978
Construction started	1985
Sales/leasing started	1987
Phase I completed	Spring 1992

Information Contact

Urban Redevelopment Authority of Pittsburgh
200 Ross Street
Pittsburgh, Pennsylvania 15219
412-255-6560

CASE STUDY: Addison Circle
Addison, Texas

Smart Growth Characteristics

⊙ Mixed-use development

⊙ Public/private partnership

⊙ Traditional neighborhood design

Smart Growth Challenges

⊙ Need for public education

⊙ High construction costs

**At about 75 dwelling units per acre (net),
Addison Circle is three times as dense as the
typical north Dallas garden apartment project.**

The Project

Addison is a traditional suburb located northwest of Dallas, Texas. Like many
edge cities, this town of 12,300 people consists primarily of commercial/business
parks; low-density residential areas; parks, schools, and other public facilities;
and strip shopping centers. Although the town is landlocked and about 80 percent built out, one of Addison's few remaining sites proved to be ideally suited for
a higher-density, mixed-use project—a radical concept for a city dominated by
conventional suburban development. Yet it was the community, through a comprehensive planning process in 1991 and, more recently, during a citizen-led
visioning exercise, that expressed the need for this form of development. The site,
which is controlled by a single landowner, is strategically located within walking
distance of employment, retail, and entertainment; it is adjacent to a Dallas Area
Rapid Transit (DART) station and close to Addison's conference and theater center. Encouraged by city officials, the landowner, Gaylord Properties, teamed with
Post Properties, an Atlanta-based REIT, to develop a plan for site.

Addison Circle's master plan establishes two subareas: a residential neighborhood of mid-rise housing with supporting retail amenities and a higher-density
office and commercial district adjacent to the North Dallas Tollway. Linking the

Many sidewalks and crosswalks are paved in brick and lined with mature shade trees, planted at 25-foot intervals.

two areas is a traffic roundabout (Addison Circle) and an axial green. Ultimately, Addison Circle will contain almost 3,000 dwelling units (mostly rental units), intermixed with neighborhood retail, ten acres of public parks, and civic space, as well as 1 million square feet of office space. At about 75 dwelling units per acre (net), the project is three times as dense as the typical north Dallas garden apartment project.

The attention to public space is one of the things that makes Addison Circle so appealing. While the circle is the symbolic center of the project, it also serves a functional role by calming traffic. A large blue sculpture at the center of the circle, the result of a design competition, has established the circle as the focal point of the project. Substantial investment is evident in the treatment of Addison Circle's residential streets and boulevards as well. Many sidewalks and crosswalks are paved in brick and lined with mature shade trees, planted at 25-foot intervals. Bicycle racks, benches, litter containers, and other street furniture add to the usability of the pedestrian-friendly public space.

Courtyards are the central gathering place for most of the residential buildings. Apartments are located along both sides of an interior corridor, with major entries and windows looking out over the street, as well as to the interior pool and courtyard areas. Some units open directly onto one of the several small parks that are interspersed throughout the neighborhood. Low stone walls edge the parks in places, defining pedestrian walkways between park and building. Hiking and biking trails are being developed, and a large area of open space has been dedicated to the town for town-sponsored events.

Addison Circle offers a wide range of housing types, ranging from 570-square-foot efficiency apartments that rent for as little as $645 per month to 3,200-square-foot lofts that rent for nearly $4,000 a month. While most of the units (45 percent) are one-bedroom models, the planned mix also includes two- and three-bedroom units, townhouses, lofts, and live/work units. The market for these units is an emerging one: those who rent by choice, not by necessity. Addison Circle residents are largely double-income couples, young childless professionals, and empty nesters, ranging in age from 25 to 55.

Addison Circle has successfully applied traditional planning and development concepts, such as placing residential units above shops and restaurants, integrating community pocket parks throughout neighborhoods, providing a human-scale pedestrian experience, and offering housing for a mix of income levels, all

A citizen-led visioning process initiated the development of Addison Circle.

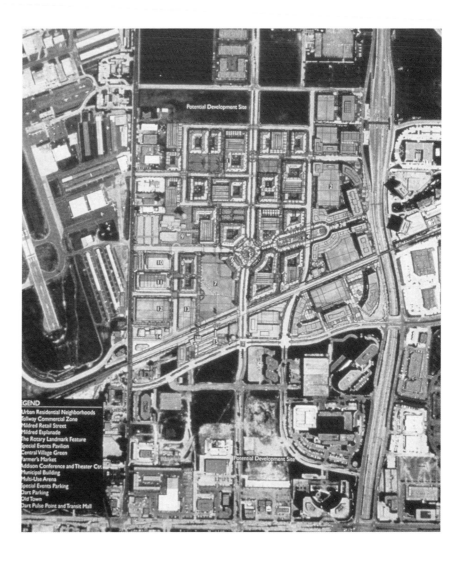

in a nontraditional location—the suburbs. It has created a town center for Addison, Texas, that is reminiscent of main streets from years gone by. "Every time I go to Addison Circle, I see someone I know," explains Carmen Moran, director of development services for the town of Addison. "It has matured into a true live, work, and play community."

Smart Growth Characteristics

Mixed-Use Development

Mixed-use development is growing in popularity in the Dallas area; with the success of Addison Circle, this trend is not likely to falter. Phase I, completed in 1997, includes 460 dwelling units, 20,000 square feet of retail space, and a half-acre park. Phase II, completed in 2000, includes 610 apartments, 90,000 square feet of retail space, 340,000 square feet of office space, and a 1.5-acre park, plus five for-sale single-family houses. A total of eight phases are planned, with an expected buildout between 2003 and 2005.

Within the large-scale commercial portion of Addison Circle, one high-rise commercial building and a mixed-use mid-rise building have been completed. The remaining phases of this sector are expected to include corporate housing and other residential uses plus office and retail space. Ultimately, 10,000 jobs will be located in the commercial portion of Addison Circle.

Public/Private Partnership

Addison Circle's public/private partnership started when the town of Addison approached the landlord, Gaylord Properties, and encouraged the firm to develop a mixed-use town center on the 80-acre parcel. This city-initiated action was a result of a community-based Vision 2020 process that recommended the development of a higher-density project on the site. Gaylord Properties and its partner, Post Properties, worked with the city and the general public to hammer out a set of design and development standards. These standards later were codified as an urban center district. The town of Addison then committed $9.5 million out of its general funds over the life of the project to support infrastructure costs, including roads and open space improvements.

Traditional Neighborhood Design

Both the architecture and site planning of Addison Circle (which was designed by Baltimore-based RTKL Associates, in conjunction with Post Properties) contribute to the community's urban texture. Most residential buildings are four stories high; in some cases, three residential levels are located above ground-floor shops and small service businesses. The modern building designs are domesticated by balconies and bays, gables and brick. Residential buildings typically rise from a stone base, which is topped by a red brick facade. Several types of window elements, including large bay windows painted to contrast with the brickwork, create architectural diversity.

Reversing the typical suburban norm of deep building setbacks and narrow sidewalks, the residential building facades at Addison Circle are set close to the street (just six feet from the sidewalk and 18 feet from the curb) and sidewalks are a generous 12 feet deep. Other new urbanist design elements, including a pedestrian-friendly street grid, pocket parks, and an axial green, contribute to the quality of life of the community—a key issue in satisfying the needs of the market segment targeted for Addison Circle.

Smart Growth Challenges

Need for Public Education

To develop a project like Addison Circle—one that is radically different and much denser than typical suburban rental projects—the developer and the town had to educate local officials and the public to the benefits of the design and establish the terms of the public/private partnership. In addition to the more typical public workshops, city staff traveled as far as Chicago and Boston to observe and measure streets and setbacks in several universally admired older urban neighborhoods.

High Construction Costs

The developer identified funding gaps that needed to be resolved in order to provide the infrastructure and level of quality mutually desired by the town and the developer. The project required heavy public subsidies to achieve economic success. "It [took] an awful lot of money to build Addison, but unlike other developments, Addison Circle will be there 100 years from now," notes Art Lomenick, executive vice president for development at Post Properties.

Project Data

Land Uses

Site area	80 acres
Gross residential density	54.6 units per acre

Land Use Plan

Use	Existing	Planned	Total
Residential (number of units)			
Apartments	1,070	1,700	2,770
Single-family houses	5	25	30
Office (square feet)	340,000	660,000	1 million
Retail (square feet)	110,000	140,000	250,000
Open space/parks (acres)	8	2	10
Total GLA (square feet)	1,354,000	2,146,000–2,646,000	3,500,000–4,000,000

Dwelling Unit Data

Type	Size (in square feet)	Current Rents
Efficiency	570–772	$645–$789
One-bedroom	681–1,079	$800–$1,220
Two-bedroom	870–1,521	$1,013–$2,015
Three-bedroom	1,570	$1,591
Loft	807–3,219	$870–$4,400

Other Data

Office occupancy rate	100%
Retail occupancy rate	85%

Development Schedule

Phase I	1997
Phase II	2000
Phase III (construction started)	2000
Buildout (expected)	2003–2005

Information Contact

Post Properties
4401 Northside Parkway
Suite 800
Atlanta, Georgia 30327
404-846-5000

CASE STUDY: Bethesda Row
Bethesda, Maryland

Smart Growth Characteristics

⊙ Mixed-use development

⊙ Transit- and pedestrian-oriented design

⊙ Town center

⊙ Public/private partnership

Smart Growth Challenges

⊙ Regulatory barriers

⊙ Public opposition

Federal Realty renovated and retenanted several existing retail facilities while constructing a new building to house the bookseller Barnes and Noble.

The Project

Bethesda Row is a multiphase, "main street," mixed-use redevelopment project in the heart of Bethesda's central business district. Bethesda, a first-ring suburb located immediately northwest of Washington, D.C., has one of the highest median household incomes in the United States. The first three phases of Bethesda Row have been completed, the fourth is currently under construction, and the fifth is being planned. The existing three phases feature 110,000 square feet of office space, 190,000 square feet of retail space, and 40,000 square feet of restaurant space, plus parking and extensive streetscape improvements. The project, which is being developed by Federal Realty Investment Trust, has helped turn this formerly neglected part of Bethesda's downtown into an attractive and vital addition to the community. Bethesda Row has been so successful that Federal Realty is employing the same development concept in other projects around the country.

Federal Realty had the good fortune of finding that the Bethesda Row site—which covers five contiguous city blocks in downtown Bethesda—was largely in the

One of the developer's biggest accomplishments was convincing regulators to permit the placement of restaurant patios next to the curb, with sidewalks adjacent to the storefronts.

hands of one private landowner. Previous uses on the site included everything from warehouses, an auto scrapyard, and a cement plant to low-rise medical office buildings and "mom and pop" retailers.

In Phase I, Federal Realty renovated and retenanted several existing retail facilities while constructing a new building to house the bookseller Barnes and Noble. It also undertook major streetscape improvements, including the addition of brick sidewalks and a fountain. The developer paid close attention to small details, going so far as to custom design attractive manhole covers for the sidewalks. When Phase I opened in June 1997, Bethesda Row was well received by the community, and since then it has come to serve as a neighborhood focal point and gathering place.

Phase II involved the renovation of existing retail space, while Phase III consisted of new construction. In both of these phases, Federal Realty continued its successful streetscape improvements. The company also sought to make the buildings appear less like superblocks and more like city blocks that had evolved naturally over time. The design process for both phases therefore involved multiple architects (with Atlanta-based Cooper Carry as the primary architect) and a conscious effort to visually differentiate various components of the buildings. The result, in all phases, has been an outstanding streetscape of great visual interest and a genuinely urban feel.

Smart Growth Characteristics

Mixed-Use Development
The multiple uses at Bethesda Row contribute to the project's success by mutually supporting each other. For instance, local office workers patronize the restaurants, while people from the wider area who make a special trip to Bethesda Row restaurants also shop at the stores. By providing a variety of people with a host of reasons to come to Bethesda Row at different times of the day and evening, the mixture of uses contributes to the project's vitality and sense of place. Federal Realty has reinforced this mix of uses with each new phase. Phase IV, for example, will include entertainment uses, such as an eight-screen art film theater, and the developer is considering mixed-density residential uses for Phase V. These uses will further enhance the urbanity of the area while also contributing to the project's financial success.

Transit- and Pedestrian-Oriented Design

Federal Realty went beyond Montgomery County planning codes requirements to create an outstanding urban environment for pedestrians. For example, the company planted larger street trees than the code required, and put considerable effort into ensuring that storefronts and building facades were differentiated from each other, significantly improving the visual interest of the streetscape.

One of Federal Realty's biggest accomplishments was convincing regulators to permit the placement of restaurant patios next to the curb, with sidewalks adjacent to the storefronts, rather than the other way around. This configuration not only does a better job of supporting the retailers, but creates a pleasant pedestrian environment. Putting this design into place involved devising a reciprocal easement with the county to allow a public easement next to the stores and an easement for Federal Realty to use the space next to the curb.

The pedestrian environment is supported by a 922-space, county-built parking structure located in the middle of the Bethesda Row project. This, along with on-street parking, provides visitors with convenient parking without creating the unpleasant "moonscape" of parking lots commonly found in suburban areas. Finally, Bethesda Row's pedestrian environment is easily accessible by public transit.

Town Center

At Bethesda Row, Federal Realty took structures and uses that were out of date and no longer compatible with the city's vision for its downtown area and updated them to meet the needs of today's residents. The project has proven exceptionally popular with the local population as a place to shop, dine, or merely stroll; it also has brought increased attention to downtown Bethesda as a destination, further contributing to the area's economic success. The county's comprehensive master plan for downtown Bethesda, the area's designation as a "designated growth area" under Maryland's smart growth legislation, and Federal Realty's energy and quality of development have demonstrated that it is possible to bring the benefits of urban living to a suburban location.

Public/Private Partnership

One unusual feature of Bethesda Row concerns its parking facilities. Nearly all of the parking for the project is provided in the county-owned garage and in county-owned surface lots, with some metered street parking. Many years ago, Montgomery County established a parking lot district for the Bethesda central business district, in which the county builds parking facilities that users then pay for on an hourly or daily basis. These facilities also are supported by a surtax on property tax assessments for properties that do not provide their own parking. This allows the owners of smaller buildings to avoid having to provide their own on-site parking, and also ensures that the area's parking spaces are efficiently operated and managed.

Smart Growth Challenges

Regulatory Barriers

While the county's master plan for downtown Bethesda did establish the framework within which Bethesda Row could be developed, it also created some barriers to the development of the district, particularly regarding transportation and streetscape improvements. The county's traffic models and standards dictated that there was insufficient capacity to support the proposed project, despite the fact that the county's master plan called for the development of additional mixed-use infill projects on sites such as this one. As a result, Federal Realty had to spend considerable time addressing these traffic standards. Similarly, the county had a very specific streetscape concept for the downtown area, which regulated everything from paving materials to trash containers. Again, Federal Realty had to convince the regulators that its development concept would provide an attractive streetscape that was also in touch with the realities of what the market wanted. The lesson that emerges is that local development regulations do not need to be rigidly calibrated and applied to ensure top-quality development; they must be sufficiently flexible to allow for successful infill development projects.

Public Opposition

When Federal Realty first proposed developing Bethesda Row, many local residents were concerned about the impact that the project would have on their community. They were particularly worried that Bethesda Row would drive local retailers out of business, replacing them with the same national retailers that can be found at any suburban mall. Federal Realty addressed this concern by meeting with local residents to discuss their ideas for the development, and by demonstrating through its leasing strategy that the residents' fears were unfounded. Indeed, Federal Realty has managed to attract an intriguing mix of local, regional, and national retailers that has succeed in generating considerable customer traffic while still providing a unique shopping experience. Residents now appreciate the fact that Bethesda Row is a major improvement on the uses that previously existed on the site.

Lessons Learned

⊙ Despite their risks and potentially higher costs, large-scale mixed-use infill developments with a strong pedestrian orientation can be very successful, even in suburban locations.

⊙ While a supportive regulatory framework is necessary for developments like Bethesda Row, regulations must be sufficiently flexible to allow developments with unique identities that can respond to ever-changing market conditions.

⊙ Developers must work closely with the community and with regulators to design program concepts that are responsive to all stakeholder needs while still ensuring that the project is financially feasible.

Project Data

Land Uses
(in square feet, unless otherwise indicated)

Use	Existing	Planned	Total
Office	110,000	80,000	190,000
Retail	190,000	110,000	300,000
Restaurant	40,000	20,000	60,000
Residential	NA	100,000	00,000
Total GLA	340,000	310,000	650,000
Parking*	450 spaces	290 spaces	740 spaces

* Parking totals do not include public on-street and garage parking available in the vicinity.

Other Data for Existing Phases

Office

Occupancy rate	99%
Number of tenants	24
Average tenant size	4,308 square feet
Annual rents	$20 to $35 per square foot
Average length of lease	Five to ten years

Retail

Occupancy rate	97%
Annual rents	$30 to $60 per square foot
Average annual sales	Approximately $400 per square foot
Average length of lease	Five to seven years

Phase III Development Costs*

Predevelopment costs	$100,000
Site improvement costs	$1,110,000
Construction costs	$5,150,000
Soft costs	$2,240,000
Total	$8,600,000

* Phase III is the smallest and most recent component.

Phase III Development Schedule

Planning started	Spring 1997
Leasing started	Fall 1997
Site leased	Fall 1998
Construction started	Fall 1998
Construction completed	October 1999

Information Contact

Federal Realty Investment Trust
1626 East Jefferson Street
Rockville, Maryland 20852
301-998-8100

CASE STUDY: Harbor Town
Memphis, Tennessee

Smart Growth Characteristics

⊙ Mixed-use development

⊙ Traditional neighborhood design

⊙ Open space protection

Smart Growth Challenges

⊙ Untested market

⊙ Regulatory barriers

Memphis's Pyramid Arena offers a contrasting
backdrop to Harbor Town's traditionally
designed neighborhoods and streets.

The Project

Harbor Town is one of the older—and most successful—new urbanist communities. The 135-acre master-planned project is located on Mud Island, virtually in
the shadow of downtown Memphis. Now mostly built out, Harbor Town's streetscape evokes the traditional town, with gridded streets, a strong pedestrian orientation, formally planned squares, and architectural forms based on historical pro-
totypes. Like many older towns, it contains a mix of housing types; one can find
$800-per-month rentals just a few steps from $800,000 riverfront homes.

A natural buildup of sand along the eastern bank of the Mississippi River created
Mud Island early in the 20th century. During the 1960s, U.S. Army Corps of Engineers dredging operations raised the island above the 100-year floodplain. The
island remained largely undeveloped, however, until the mid-1980s, when a
bridge connecting it with downtown Memphis was built. Developers Henry Turley
and Jack Belz acquired the Harbor Town site in 1987.

After more than a decade of development, 850 of Harbor Town's dwelling units
have been completed. About half of the units built are for-sale housing (mostly
single-family detached houses); the remainder are rental apartments. (Harbor

Town's apartments have been especially successful, with average rents reaching $0.90 per square foot, compared with a Memphis area average of $0.75.) The community also contains a Montessori school, a 50-slip marina, and a mixed-use town center with shops, services, and a 6,500-square-foot grocery store. A yacht club and office space, along with high-end condominiums, are expected to finish out the town center by the end of 2001.

As Harbor Town enters the last stages of its buildout, empirical evidence demonstrates that the homebuying public recognizes its special design qualities. *Valuing the New Urbanism,* a 1999 ULI publication, reports that Harbor Town has achieved a 25 percent price premium relative to other housing in its market, a premium that is attributable to the community's design.

Smart Growth Characteristics

Mixed-Use Development

Harbor Town has successfully integrated a mixture of housing types—including single-family detached houses, townhouses, apartments, and condominiums—to achieve an overall gross density of 7.40 units per acre. According to town architect J. Carson Looney, this variety of lot sizes, unit types, and costs has helped to capture an unserved and important market segment. With its commercial/retail town center and a network of parks and trails, Harbor Town also encourages pedestrian activity and reduces residents' dependence on the automobile.

Traditional Neighborhood Design

Memphis, Tennessee–based Looney Ricks Kiss Architects (LRK) established visual guidelines to set the basic ground rules for street facades, scale and proportion, materials, and key details. In support of the traditional architectural vernacular, these guidelines require, for example, that windows be oriented vertically, rather than horizontally, and that porches be raised 24 to 30 inches above grade. In addition to establishing an overall aesthetic for the community, the design guidelines ensure that lower-priced homes maintain a level of design compatible in quality to the more expensive ones—a key to successful sales price mixing, according to Looney.

While 12 different architects have designed houses for some 20 different builders at Harbor Town, LRK has designed about 65 percent of the community's single-family units and townhouses. Most of the residential designs are updates of local vernacular forms, ranging from Charleston side-yard homes to simple shotgun

WOLF RIVER

MISSISSIPPI RIVER

cottages, although some units are more modern in detail. The small-lot designs by LRK are among the most interesting and innovative. Situated on lots as small as 25 to 30 feet by 90 to 110 feet, these houses are typically side-yard designs, one room (occasionally two rooms) wide, with alley garages. Many of these houses have raised front porches and second-story balconies to engage the street.

Open Space Protection

The site plan for Harbor Town, designed by Baltimore-based RTKL Associates, is composed of a series of radial boulevards superimposed on a grid of blocks. The boulevards open the interior of the site to views of the Mississippi River and the downtown skyline. They—and other major streets—terminate at neighborhood parks, which provide a visual and psychological focus for Harbor Town's individual neighborhoods. A wetlands detention feature running through the center of the site is designed to look like a stream and ponds. A three-mile-long nature/jogging trail that also includes several seating areas also runs through the town. The town center, located toward the community's southern edge, continues the formal system of radials and focal points. Smaller residential lots are oriented toward neighborhood parks so that they, in essence, "borrow" the communal open space. (Although they lacking river views, the lots across from the neighborhood parks sold quickly and commanded premium prices.)

Smart Growth Challenges

Untested Market

Builders and buyers initially questioned the viability of a residential community in downtown Memphis, at a time when most new growth was occurring on the eastern side of the metropolitan area—not adjacent to downtown. It took considerable effort and expense to persuade builders to construct houses speculatively, and to persuade realtors to bring prospective buyers to see them. Expecting that sales to families would be among the most difficult to close—given the poor reputation of the local public schools—the developer initially offered lot price concessions of $1,200 per child. An on-site Montessori school also was established; it already has been expanded three times. Through these efforts, and through the design of the community itself, Harbor Town has won over a substantial number of families with children. Overall, given the variety of housing sizes and prices offered, the project has attracted a wide spectrum of buyers, including empty nesters, single people, and professional couples as well as families.

Regulatory Barriers

Designed to create a more intimate and pedestrian-scaled community, Harbor Town's streets are gridded, narrow, and short, and building setbacks are minimized. Local street rights-of-way are 44 feet wide, with a 28-foot curb-to-curb distance, including parking on both sides of the street. The traffic-calming effect of this streetscape is evident. "It is difficult to drive more than 35 miles an hour almost anywhere in the community," Looney notes. During the approval process, the city refused to accept ownership of the narrow streets, requiring Harbor Town's streets to be private. However, after years of proof that such streets create a more livable environment, Harbor Town's standards have become a model for public streets elsewhere in Memphis.

Lessons Learned

⊙ Never underestimate the conservatism of American homebuyers. To overcome the market's predisposition to the norm, the marketing budget for Harbor Town is several times larger than what would be considered typical.

⊙ When undertaking an unusual project in an unproven location, recognize that the mathematical probability of achieving a sale is small. Often, one member of a household has been willing to purchase at Harbor Town, but another has not. In virtually all of these cases, the sale was lost.

⊙ Do not underestimate the number of families with children who are willing to live downtown. Harbor Town's private school and special promotions to families have been factors in its success, but it is the project's design that ultimately proved most important in attracting traditional families.

Project Data

Land Uses

Site area	135 gross acres
Dwelling units completed/planned	850/1,000
Gross density	7.40 units per acre
Net density	9.6 units per acre
Lot sizes	2,500–7,000 square feet
Parking	1,750 spaces
Parking ratio	2 spaces/unit (plus on-street parking)

Land Use Plan

Use	Acres	Percent of Site
Residential	70.5	52%
Recreation/amenities	9.0	7%
Roads/parking	21.0	16%
Open space	27.0	20%
Other	7.5	5%
Total	135	100%

Development Costs

Type	Total Cost
Site acquisition costs	$2,251,470
Site improvement costs	$1,750,000
Construction costs	$6,550,000
Soft costs	$5,500,000
Total	$16,051,470

Dwelling Unit Data

Type	Size (in square feet)	Number Planned/Built	Sales Prices/Rents
Single-family house	1,300–6,500	396/351	$115,000–$1,000,000
Attached townhouse	1,200–1,700	35/35	$120,000–$180,000
Apartment	630–1,500	420/420	$550–$1,200
Condominium	1,200–2,400	24/12	$250,000–$350,000

Information Contact

Henry Turley Company
65 Union Avenue, Suite 1200
Memphis, Tennessee 38103
901-527-2770

CASE STUDY: Phillips Place
Charlotte, North Carolina

Smart Growth Characteristics

◉ Town center

◉ Pedestrian-oriented design

Smart Growth Challenges

◉ Regulatory barriers

◉ Site constraints

◉ Public opposition

Phillips Place combines ground-level retail with apartments above in a traditional suburban setting.

The Project

Phillips Place is a suburban mixed-use development featuring 130,000 square feet of retail space, 402 residential units, 124 hotel rooms, and a multiplex cinema. Located 20 minutes south of downtown Charlotte, the project includes a pedestrian-scaled main street within a traditional low-density suburban area. The three-story buildings on this street feature ground-level retail uses with apartments above. The classically influenced architecture and the significant emphasis on high-quality streetscape design and lighting combine to create a pleasant and safe pedestrian experience.

The 32-acre site is located approximately 15 to 20 minutes from the airport and the outer loop beltway in rapidly developing SouthPark. It was the last remaining site with retail potential in the area. SouthPark itself is home to the Carolinas' second-largest business district and its residents have one of the highest income levels in the southeast.

The challenge of this project was to develop a thriving, mixed-use town center for a traditionally low-density suburban business district and residential neighbor-

hood. The developer—the Harris Company—sought to achieve this goal by creating a main street with a 124-room hotel anchoring one end and a multiplex cinema anchoring the other, apartments built over retail space on one side of the street, and several separate apartment buildings behind the main street. Its commercial tenants include Dean & Deluca, Via Veneto Fashion Shoes, Restoration Hardware, and Palm Restaurant.

The Harris Group partnered with Post Properties of Atlanta to construct and manage the over-the-shop apartments as well as the separate apartment buildings nearby. It chose the Charlotte-based Panos Hotel Group as a hotel partner and operator. A single construction company handled the retail, hotel, and cinema development, eliminating numerous coordination issues. Construction began in November 1995 and was completed in March 1998.

Smart Growth Characteristics

Town Center
Phillips Place combines specialty retail, entertainment, townhomes, apartments, and a hotel, all organized around a main street. It provides an important urban gathering place for the surrounding low-density suburban community and illustrates how relatively dense mixing of a variety of uses can create a sense of community in the heart of suburbia.

Pedestrian-Oriented Design
The project was designed to create a pedestrian-scaled town center by internalizing the main street in order to provide a slower, more controlled environment than the fast-moving, automobile-oriented environments of the surrounding areas. Designers emphasized landscaped features, including two courtyards that terminate at the east/west axis of the main street, streetscaping (including brick sidewalks and outdoor seating), and pleasant lighting to encourage pedestrian mobility throughout the site.

Smart Growth Challenges

Regulatory Barriers
In order to build a mixed-use development, the property had to be rezoned. The South District Plan recommended the site for multifamily housing at a density of 22 units per acre. This would have permitted 800 units on the site, which would have generated significant traffic during peak hours. The Harris Group argued

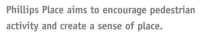

Phillips Place aims to encourage pedestrian
activity and create a sense of place.

successfully that it could reduce peak hour traffic by adding nonresidential uses.
The developer also argued that the project's retail and public spaces would serve
as valuable community amenities.

Complicating the rezoning approval process was the fact that the county lacked
a mixed-use zoning classification. To address this impediment, the Harris Group
worked closely with the city's planning staff to create a new zoning category that
would allow the integration of retail and residential uses.

Site Constraints
The site itself had several specific constraints to development, including high-
tension power lines located at the front of the property (along the arterial frontage)
and a terrain that slopes from north to south. The greatest constraint was limited
access to the site, which has substantial frontage on Fairview Road (southeast
Charlotte's major east/west thoroughfare) but is not served by any other adjacent
streets. All access, therefore, is provided along Fairview Road, a constraint that
limited the developers' and designers' ability to connect the project to its sur-
roundings.

Public Opposition
Concerns over increased traffic, especially additional traffic flowing through adjacent neighborhoods, made it impossible for the developer to connect the main
street to the surrounding neighborhoods with either vehicle or pedestrian link-
ages. While the site is separated from the adjacent residential neighborhoods by
fences, several neighborhood groups—impressed with the quality and design of
the final project—are considering ways to effectively connect their neighborhoods
to Phillips Place. While the project remains very much a suburban development
that is accessed primarily by car, original connections to the adjacent neighborhoods would have helped integrate the site into the community and reduce car
trips.

Lessons Learned

⊙ Phillips Place demonstrates how a mixed-use town center can be successfully
developed in a fast-growing suburban business district. The project provides an
important "urban" gathering place for the low-density suburban community and

illustrates how the relatively dense mixing of a variety of uses can create synergy and a whole that is greater than the sum of its parts.

⊙ Phillips Place brings to the Charlotte suburbs a new urban element, giving its residents the opportunity to walk to many conveniences and providing visitors and nearby residents and workers with an exciting combination of dining, shopping, and entertainment in one location. Phillips Place is a major step in the right direction for suburban place making and pedestrian-oriented mixed-use development.

Project Data

Land Uses

Site area	35 acres
Retail	129,394 square feet
Residential	402 units
Hotel 124 rooms	(80,000 square feet)
Parking 790 spaces	(200,000 square feet)
Percent of gross leasable area (GLA) occupied	95 percent
Annual rents	Approximately $26 to $30 per square foot
Average annual sales	Approximately $330 per square foot
Average length of lease	Five to ten years

Development Costs

Site acquisition cost	$11,950,000
Site improvement costs	$3,907,842
Parking deck	$1,700,000
Construction costs	$60,254,000
Soft costs	$2,598,825
Total	$80,410,667

Development Schedule

Site purchased	November 1995
Construction started	November 1995
Phase I completed	June 1997
Project completed	March 1998

Information Contact

The Harris Group
Rotunda Suite 175
4201 Congress Street
Charlotte, North Carolina
704-556-1717

Smart Growth Characteristics

⊙ Environmental features

⊙ Conservation design

Smart Growth Challenge

⊙ Untested market

The 2,400-acre Bonita Bay community offers single-family, villa, and coach and carriage homes, plus high-rise condominiums.

The Project

The vision for Bonita Bay began with David Shakarian, founder and original chairman of General Nutrition Corporation (GNC). In 1979, Shakarian began assembling land in southwest Florida for the development of a unique, environmentally integrated master-planned community that would set new standards in environmentally responsible development, integrating people, plants, and animals in a natural environment and preserving and enhancing the natural treasures of the Gulf Coast. After Shakarian's death in 1984, David Lucas, Shakarian's son-in-law, was named chairman of Bonita Bay Properties, Inc. (BBPI), continuing its founder's vision. The community opened for sales in 1985.

Bonita Bay is an environmentally sensitive, 2,400-acre master-planned community located along the ecologically rich Gulf Coast of southwest Florida. The primary- and second-home community offers single-family, villa, and coach and carriage homes and high-rise condominiums. Five private championship golf courses, two golf clubhouses, 18 tennis courts, three waterfront parks, a gulf beach park, a marina, and miles of secluded walking and biking paths are among the community's offerings.

Preserving and enhancing the area's natural, historical, and archaeological features was the guiding principle in developing Bonita Bay. The community's intimate neighborhoods were planned around the area's natural topography and vegetation. Wherever possible, the site's natural flora and fauna were left undis-

Wetlands and native vegetation are used to filter nutrients, silt, and other pollutants, and natural wildlife areas have been conserved to protect water quality and habitat.

turbed, resulting in a community whose natural landscaping Bonita Bay Properties vice president Ed Rodgers describes as "the real Florida." To maintain this authenticity, the community requires that all landscaping schemes incorporate at least 50 percent native vegetation.

Management of the community also fosters the preservation and enhancement of the natural terrain. The community's golf courses are included in the Audubon Cooperative Sanctuary Program for Golf Courses and in the Audubon International Signature Program. Old specimen pine trees have been fitted with copper lightning rods for their protection, and hundreds of oaks were relocated throughout the community.

Smart Growth Characteristics

Environmental Features

In 1981, a team of planners, environmental engineers, archaeologists, and other consultants was formed to prepare an impact assessment report for development of the land. This intensive process identified 40 different habitat types and mapped 22 different drainage basins. BBPI's master plan for the area preserved natural wetlands and called for the creation of a stormwater management system that employs native vegetation to filter out silt, nutrients, and pollutants. The plan also employed an innovative and sophisticated dual-delivery water management system to supply both potable and irrigation water to homes and treated effluent to irrigate the golf course. To further conserve water, the plan adopted xeriscaping principles, which call for use of mostly native plants that require minimal watering.

The community's water management system employs natural filtration to control and filter stormwater runoff. The sophisticated system, which was named the 1985 Civil Engineering Project of the Year in South Florida, follows the natural contours of the land. The dual-line water system supplies both potable water and water to irrigate the golf courses and landscaping, which is drawn from treated effluent and well water. A network of weather stations throughout the community monitors golf course conditions and irrigates only those areas that need water.

Land for development was cleared selectively in order to preserve specimen tree stands and important archaeological and ecological sites. Natural wildlife areas were conserved by restricting construction vehicles and equipment to old hunting trails, and ancient Native American shell mounds were left undisturbed.

Conservation Design

One-half of the community will remain as open space. In addition to golf, the community boasts three waterfront parks: a historical/archaeological park with a boardwalk leading into Estero Bay, a nature retreat that includes a canoe launching area and hiking trails, and a third park that provides a boat launch, a fitness trail, and open space that can accommodate large communitywide functions. In 1987, an additional off-site, private, gulf-front beach park for residents opened on Bonita Beach. Shuttle buses transport residents to the parks and other areas of the community and to the off-site beach, and 12 miles of bicycle paths connect the entire community.

Smart Growth Challenge

Untested Market

The desirability of Bonita Bay and its array of amenities has challenged the developer to maintain the master plan's original intent—to create an environmentally responsible community that integrates people, places, plants, and animals in a natural state. Development was carefully phased to respond to market demand. As buildout of the community continued, BPPI realized a higher level of golf membership participation than was typical of golf communities at the time; about half the homebuyers were purchasing golf club memberships, and they tended to be more serious golfers. It became apparent that a second course would be required. The master plan was amended, taking land planned for commercial and more residential development for an additional golf course. In 1991, the Creekside golf course opened.

Bonita Bay also steadily attracted more affluent buyers, who appreciated the community's unique environment and its high-quality services and amenities. In 1991, along with the second golf course, the community opened a tennis and pool complex. In 1995, the tennis center was expanded to 13 courts, and in 1996 a 3,500-square-foot fitness center was opened.

BBPI adjusted subsequent development phases to meet the demands of its new, more affluent homebuyers, incorporating more and larger single-family lots in new residential sections and providing for more open space. The initial, approved master plan called for development of 9,240 units; in response to market demand, this figure has been reduced significantly, to fewer than 3,300 units at buildout.

The immense market demand to live and play in the community also has affected the project's affordability. Home prices range from $145,000 to more than $2 million. Current market demand stands in stark contrast to early market studies, which suggested that a community of moderately priced houses (initial lot prices in the community averaged $75,000) with relatively modest amenities be developed on the site. This recommendation has proven to be wrong, as lots and homes exceed price expectations and the number of amenities continues to rise.

Project Data

Land Uses

Site area	2,425 acres
Dwelling units completed/planned	2,436/3,300
Gross density	1.4 units per acre
Average net density	3.0 units per acre

Land Use Plan

Use	Acres	Percent of Site
Detached residential	331.7	14%
Attached/multifamily residential	744.6	31%
Golf courses	550	22%
Roads	102	4%
Common open space/parks	36.6	2%
Reserve/slough	589	24%
Commercial	69.9	3%
Total	2,423.8	100%

Development Costs

Site acquisition cost	$17,000,000
Site improvement costs	$68,000,000 (includes golf course construction)
Building construction costs	$18,500,000
Soft costs	$56,500,000
Total (as of mid-2000)	$143,000,000 (excludes land costs)

Development Schedule

Site purchased	1979–1980
Planning started (DRI approved)	November 1981
Construction started (golf course)	1983
Sales started	1985
First closing	1985
Phase I completed	1985
Buildout (projected)	2006

Information Contact

Bonita Bay Properties, Inc.
3451 Bonita Bay Boulevard
Suite 202
Bonita Springs, Florida 34134
941-495-1000

CASE STUDY: Fairview Village
Fairview, Oregon

Smart Growth Characteristics

⊙ Collaborative planning

⊙ Pedestrian-oriented design

Smart Growth Challenges

⊙ Regulatory barriers

⊙ Untested market

Developing the Fairview Village site as a traditional village, rather than as a single-use residential subdivision, required revisions to local codes and ordinances.

The Project

Developer Rick Holt, president of Portland-based Holt and Haugh, Inc., set out to create a community that reflected the architectural design and produced the "sense of place" reminiscent of traditional towns. The result of his vision is Fairview Village, a 95-acre project that integrates a mix of residential development with commercial and civic buildings, includes parks and open spaces, and is pedestrian oriented. The project is located within the city of Fairview, Oregon, which is 20 minutes east of downtown Portland. "Fairview Village is a town in the classic sense—a coherent neighborhood built around a commercial center, anchored by civic buildings and public parks, scaled to people rather than to their cars," explains Sarah Holt, vice president, Holt and Haugh.

In 1994, Holt and Haugh purchased part of a 137-acre site from Tektronix, a locally based high-tech firm. (The remainder of the Tektronix property was dedicated to the community as a park and a site for an elementary school; the school, which is located less than one-quarter of a mile from Fairview Village, was completed in 1997.) Developing the site in a traditional village design, rather than as a single-use residential subdivision, required revisions to local codes and ordinances. Ironically, while the village concept was not permitted under existing land use regulations, the city preferred it to previous development proposals, which included shopping centers and large-lot subdivisions. In designing the site, Holt and

At buildout, the village will contain 405 residential units, including single-family houses, rowhouses, condominiums, apartments, and duplexes.

Haugh conducted a public participation process, which led to a conceptual plan that reflected the developer's vision and the community's interests.

Fairview Village is currently in the final phase of a seven-phase development process that began in 1995. As of mid-2000, 405 residential units—including single-family houses, rowhouses, condominiums, apartments, and duplexes—have been constructed. To complement that residential development, Fairview Village includes a U.S. Post Office that will anchor the planned retail town center, a 34,000-square-foot Gold's Gym, and a La Petite Academy (one of a national chain of daycare centers). The developer established relatively strict design guidelines to ensure that the community's buildings reflect the architectural style of the city of Fairview's "old town" section. The site also includes nearly 16 acres of open space, which is connected by trails and bridges to a 40-acre park and natural area located directly adjacent to the project. Convenient public transportation opportunities exist near Fairview Village. Bus stops are located on both the north/south and east/west arterials immediately adjacent to the project, and a Tri-Met MAX light-rail line is located one and one-half miles south of Fairview Village. (Light-rail passengers can get to downtown Portland in approximately 35 minutes.)

The project's final phase is expected to be completed by spring 2002. At buildout, the site will include more than 550 residential units, 140,000 square feet of commercial space, 200,000 square feet of retail space, 30,000 square feet of civic space, ten parks, and a system of walking trails.

Smart Growth Characteristics

Collaborative Planning

Nearly 100 community stakeholders—including city officials, architects, builders, bankers, and area residents—participated in a three-day charrette to produce a development plan that encompasses a broad range of community design expectations. Engaging the public and private sector in this collaborative process was critical to advancing the project. "The process established a core set of architectural principles, a master plan for the site, and a regulating plan," explains developer Holt. "More importantly, it provided an opportunity for everyone in the community to understand each other's points of view." Indeed, the charrette process is credited for getting the public officials' support to revise codes and permit the village development approach.

Pedestrian-Oriented Design

Several design devices reinforce Fairview Village's pedestrian orientation. Holt and Haugh held residential street widths to a minimum and used street paving as a traffic calming device at intersections. To further enhance pedestrian opportunities, Fairview Village's site design provides for alley-accessed parking, which moved garages to the rear of homes and eliminated excessive numbers of curb cuts and driveways. The community's single-family houses, which architecturally reflect the vernacular of the city of Fairview's historic homes, are set close to the street and typically include front porches. The shallow setback requirements and the addition of front porches create a more active, pedestrian-oriented street life. The community's narrow, tree-lined streets and wide sidewalks further enhance its walkability. Pedestrian bridges, built by Holt and Haugh, also connect residents to adjacent parks and the elementary school.

Smart Growth Challenges

Regulatory Barriers

Holt and Haugh had to overcome a series of regulatory barriers to create a smart growth community. When the project was conceived, government codes and ordinances encouraged typical suburban patterns of development—houses set far back from the road, on large lots, with commercial and residential uses separated—and discouraged the neighborhood design necessary for the developer's vision to be achieved.

To overcome these barriers, Holt and Haugh set out to reform local policies so that smart growth development could take place. Working with the local government, the developer prepared a planned unit development code that allowed for a mix of uses, reduced or eliminated housing setbacks, and permitted home offices. "Ideally, we would have changed the city's codes so that smart growth development such as ours would be the preferred development zone in the city," says Holt.

Untested Market

The market for a mixed-use, higher-density development (with an average lot size of approximately 5,500 square feet) in the small city of Fairview (population 3,800) was unknown. Conventional wisdom and market studies suggested that the 95-acre site was better suited for a standard subdivision—single residential use on larger lots—than for a mixed-use project. But because there were no analogous projects in the area, Holt felt that conventional market analysis did not reflect the emerging markets that favored this form of development. "Market studies generally focus on past performance rather than on future trends," notes Holt. The developer sought to reach a middle-income market of empty nesters, double-income professional couples, and young families. While sales were slow at the beginning, the pace of sales increased over time.

Lessons Learned

⊙ Alternative financing options should always be explored. Instead of appraising the content of the entire project, the banks that Fairview Village's developer worked with accepted appraisals on isolated lots only. This approach reduced appraisal values by 15 percent.

⊙ Developers should adhere to the original design intent of the community's master plan. The temptation to divert from the plan may be strong if sales are not initially brisk or if retailers demand certain concessions. The result could be a piecemeal subdivision that lacks the character and design qualities that drew initial buyers and leasers to the project in the first place.

Project Data

Land Uses

Type	Acres	Percent of Site
Buildings	49.46	52%
Streets/surface parking	27.72	29%
Landscaping/open space	9.1	10%
Other (easement, creeks)	8.72	9%
Total	95	100%

Land Use Plan

(Gross building area, in square feet)

Use	Existing	Planned
Office	32,500	207,500
Retail	0	150,000
Residential	604,800	785,000
Recreation	33,000	33,000
Parking	130,000	565,000
Other (medical)	0	5,000
Total	800,300	1,745,500

Dwelling Unit Data

Type	Floor Area (in square feet)	Number	Initial Price Range
Single-family detached	2,000	126	$135,000–$375,000
Single-family attached	2,500	14	$230,000–$301,000
Rowhouse	1,500	68	$145,000–$294,000
Condominium	1,000	68	$83,000–$165,000
Apartment	900	56	$660–$1,050 per month
Duplex	300	22	$990–$1,150 per month
Carriage house	500	51	$450–$650 per month

Development Costs

Site acquisition cost	$2,950,000
Site improvement costs	$14,650,000
Construction costs	
Office	$60 per square foot, plus $25 per square foot for tenant improvements
Retail	$78 per square foot
Residential	$85 per square foot
Soft costs	$2,000,000
Total	$19,650,000*

* Does not include construction costs.

Development Schedule

Site purchased	September 1994
Planning started	May 1994
Construction started	March 1995
Sales/leasing started	December 1995
Phase I completed	December 1997
Buildout (projected)	March 2002

Information Contact

Holt and Haugh, Inc.
1200 NW Front Avenue, Suite 620
Portland, Oregon 97209
www.fairviewvillage.com

CASE STUDY: Orenco Station
Hillsboro, Oregon

Smart Growth Characteristics

⊙ Transit-oriented design

⊙ Town center

⊙ Pedestrian-oriented design

Smart Growth Challenges

⊙ Untested market

⊙ Regulatory barriers

Orenco Station's town center includes three restaurants and 26,000 square feet of retail space.

The Project

Orenco Station is a pedestrian-oriented, mixed-use community planned by master developer Pacific Realty Associates, L.P. (PacTrust), for 1,834 housing units, as well as retail and office space. The compact design includes a wide range of housing types, from single-family detached houses to accessory units over garages to live/work lofts and townhouses over retail shops. The common thread of the community is a formal system of open spaces and miniparks—a "string of pearls," as the development team calls it—terminating in the recently opened Orenco Station stop of the Tri-Met MAX light-rail line connecting downtown Portland to its suburbs.

Orenco's housing units are relatively small: single-family detached models range from 1,400 to 1,940 square feet. Unit designs include two- and three-bedroom models, although flexible spaces allow some models to be converted to three- or four-bedroom residences. In response to emerging lifestyle patterns and preferences, all units include a dedicated home office space and high-speed wiring for computer communication.

Unlike more traditional subdivisions, at Orenco Station, three- and four-unit townhouse structures are integrated with single-family detached housing, and often

are set at the ends of single-family blocks. From the exterior, the townhouse structures are designed to look like larger cousins of the adjacent single-family houses, with asymmetric and varied facades and entryways.

The town center lies at the intersection of Orenco Station's north/south axis and Cornell Road, an existing major arterial road. The town center structures, designed by Portland-based Fletcher Farr Ayotte Architects, provide space for small neighborhood retail uses. Office space and housing are located on the second and third floors, above the retail space. A second retail center at the edge of the community—the Crossroads—houses a grocery, a sporting goods store, and a copy shop in approximately 130,000 square feet of space. (At buildout, this center will total approximately 500,000 square feet of retail space.)

Sales at Orenco Station have exceeded projections, according to Rudy Kadlub of Costa Pacific Homes. Absorption has averaged seven units per month, and prices as of mid-2000 are running about 20 to 30 percent above the area average. Demographically, homebuyers at Orenco Station have been primarily single people, professional couples, and empty nesters. As might be expected, given the project's small-lot/small-unit design, few have been families with children.

Smart Growth Characteristics

Transit-Oriented Design
Originally zoned for industrial use and later rezoned for subdivision housing, the present community of Orenco Station was born of the site's designation as a "town center" in the Portland Metro Area 2040 Plan. This plan established a gradient of residential density targets at varying distances from the Orenco light-rail stop and mandated mixed-use development. After two years of discussions, design studies, and negotiations with city, state, and transit officials, a custom-tailored zoning ordinance for Orenco Station was created. Dubbed a "station community residential village," or SCRV district, the new zoning established design guidelines that would allow for—and ensure—the sort of heterogeneous and urban mixing of housing types and land uses not typically found in the suburbs.

The light-rail station, located at the southern edge of Orenco Station, is a key component of the community's site design. The primary circulation network—both vehicular and pedestrian—runs axially from the station to the town center and culminates in a formal village green. Secondary circulation and open spaces branch laterally from this ceremonial spine. In addition to light rail, Orenco Station pro-

The light-rail station, located at the southern edge of Orenco Station, is a key component of the community's site design.

vides shuttle bus service that connects the community to a nearby high-tech employment center to its north.

Town Center

Cited by homeowners as community's number one amenity, Orenco Station's seven-acre town center serves as the community's central gathering place. The center's 26,000 square feet of retail space is occupied by neighborhood stores, including three restaurants (several of which offer outdoor dining along extrawide 17-foot sidewalks), a wine shop, a coffee shop, a cleaners, and a florist. Offices and loft residences are located on the town center's second and third floors; the center also includes several live/work townhouse units. Ninety percent of the town center's retail space was leased and occupied in less than one year. Of the 31,000 square feet of office space existing as of mid-2000, 70 percent is leased, with rents that are higher than those for comparably sized offices in the area.

When completed, Orenco Station's town center will include 46,000 square feet of retail space, 41,000 square feet of office space, 22 loft residences, and 28 live/work townhouse units. "It is clear that the town center's pedestrian character and the restaurants and other services it provides are an important amenity to the residents of Orenco Station," explains Mike Mehaffy of PacTrust. "In fact, there are several examples, beyond the obvious live/work homes, of business owners living in the community. The town center has truly helped nurture a sense of place in Orenco Station."

Pedestrian-Oriented Design

Several design devices reinforce Orenco Station's pedestrian and community orientation. Residential street widths were minimized (to 25 feet, with parking on one side) and sidewalks bulbed to narrow intersections and slow traffic. To further reduce the impact of the automobile, the project's site design provides for alley parking access, thereby eliminating the garage door–dominated front building elevations often found in high-density suburban communities.

Orenco Station's dwelling units are set close to the street, with eight-foot maximum setbacks for townhouses and 13- to 19-foot setbacks for detached units. Facade designs are based on Portland-area craftsman and English cottage precedents, and most have front porches. The smaller-than-typical frontyard setbacks and front porches are intended to encourage a more active and engaged street life.

Single-family lots at Orenco Station are relatively small, ranging from 3,680 to 4,500 square feet. The smallest lots are 40 feet wide. Dwelling units are positioned five feet from one side lot line, with an easement to use the five-foot yard granted to the abutting lot. The net result, incorporating the adjacent property's "passive use" easement, is a usable side yard 12 to 15 feet wide (on a 40-foot lot) running the length of the house. Pushing the unit five feet off the lot line and granting the easement provides houses with the same size side yard as a zero-lot-line unit, but with the benefit of windows on the side elevation.

Smart Growth Challenges

Untested Market

With little precedent for either higher-density *or* mixed-use development in the area, PacTrust, under the direction of CEO Peter Bechen and corporate architect Ken Grimes, assembled a team of designers, engineers, and homebuilders to explore the locally uncharted waters. They conducted market research among workers in the surrounding high-tech facilities to establish design and housing preferences and to define affordability issues. This survey and focus group research revealed an attraction to the look and feel Portland's older suburbs, with their craftsman and cottage architecture, picturesque rose gardens, and neighborhood-oriented shops. The group subsequently studied Portland's older suburban neighborhoods, noting their walkability and mixed land uses. Based on these studies and on a market analysis, the team decided that incorporating the core design and planning attributes of older communities was essential to creating an appealing and successful high-density project.

Regulatory Barriers

Local codes and regulations proved a challenge to building Orenco Station. The developer worked with the local jurisdiction to shape a new zoning ordinance that allowed for higher-density development and a pedestrian orientation, while providing the necessary flexibility to respond to market demands. Rather than following a strict density formula, which the local jurisdiction initially recommended, the developer committed to delivering a specific number of residential units, while Hillsboro officials allowed PacTrust a certain amount of flexibility in determining the configuration of those units.

Lessons Learned

⊙ Higher densities and mixed housing types can succeed in suburban markets. Success, says PacTrust and its design team, comes in large measure from the attention paid to the public spaces, which offsets any disadvantages of smaller private spaces.

⊙ Post-purchase focus groups have cited Orenco Station's community and pedestrian orientations as primary reasons for purchasing a home there.

⊙ Accessory units have been a success. Homeowners have used the space in a variety of ways, as office space, guest quarters, or small apartments. The availability of accessory units has added to the project's market appeal.

Project Data

Land Uses

Site area	61.2 acres (of a 190-acre master plan)
Dwelling units	446
Gross density	7.3 units per acre
Net density	10.85 units per acre
Lot sizes	3,680–4,500 square feet
Parking	835 spaces
Parking ratio	1.9 spaces/unit

Land Use Plan

Use	Acres	Percent of Site
Residential	30.25	49%
Recreation/amenities	1.05	2%
Roads/parking	20.1	33%
Open space	7.80	13%
Other (mixed use)	2.0	3%
Total	61.2	100%

Development Costs

Type	Total Cost	Cost per Dwelling Unit
Site acquisition cost	$5,400,000	$12,100
Site improvement cost	$12,000,000	$26,900
Construction cost	$45,800,000	$102,700
Soft costs	$13,100,000	$29,400
Total	$76,300,000	$171,100

Information Contact

Pacific Realty Associates, LP (PacTrust)
15350 SW Sequoia Parkway, Suite 300
Portland, Oregon 97224
503-624-6300

CASE STUDY: Prairie Crossing
Grayslake, Illinois

Smart Growth Characteristics

⊙ Conservation design

⊙ Environmental features

⊙ Pedestrian-oriented design

Smart Growth Challenges

⊙ Regulatory barriers

⊙ Untested market

Prairie Crossing is a unique conservation design community of 362 single-family homes located on 667 acres.

The Project

Located 45 miles north of Chicago in Grayslake, Illinois, Prairie Crossing is a unique conservation development that includes many smart growth characteristics. The community's planned 362 units will rest on a small portion of the site's 677 acres. The majority of the land is to be left as open space to protect environmental resources and the site's rural character. The community's more than 350 acres of permanent open space include 160 acres of restored prairie, 158 acres of active farmland, 13 acres of wetlands, a 22-acre lake, three ponds, a village green, and recreational parks. Prairie Crossing's open space network is the western anchor of a 2,500-acre preserved area—the Liberty Prairie Reserve—making it part of a larger protected and functioning ecosystem. Ten miles of internal trails at Prairie Crossing (which will enable residents to bike to a regional commuter rail station) eventually will connect through the reserve to the Des Plaines River trail system linking Wisconsin and Cook County.

Prairie Crossing's 362 single-family homes are located strategically to protect important natural features such as hedgerows, native habitats, and wetlands. The 1,140- to 3,428-square-foot houses, which reflect traditional midwestern farmhouse and village vernacular, are clustered in four lot types that range in size from

7,000 to 20,000 square feet. These homes, which range in price from $250,000 to $427,000, all share views of the community's protected open space.

The community has a restored 1885 barn that serves as a community center, a charter school, a stable, homeowner garden plots, and a community-supported organic farm with three farm markets weekly. Combined, these novel features create a sense of community by encouraging interaction among residents. Future plans include a modest office and mixed-use retail center adjacent to the Prairie Crossing railroad station, which provides service to downtown Chicago, O'Hare airport, and suburban offices. Sites for commercial and limited industrial adjoin the residential development on the north.

The innovative site design was a response to local government and neighborhood opposition to a high-density development originally proposed for the site. That proposal faced difficult battles in obtaining necessary development approvals. After years of lawsuits and opposition, Gaylord Donnelley, a long-time conservationist and former chairman of the R.R. Donnelley and Sons printing company, and neighbors stepped forward and purchased the property in 1987 for approximately $7,500 per acre through the newly formed Prairie Holdings Corporation.

Donnelley's nephew, George Ranney, Jr., and his wife, Victoria Post Ranney, have been involved in Prairie Holdings from the outset and now head the development group. They have developed the site using ten guiding principles that underscore the developer's commitment to protect the environment and the rural character of the region. Charles Shaw, a former ULI president, provided the initial development management through the Chicago-based Shaw Company.

The project's design features and amenities are creating value in the marketplace. According to a 1999 marketing analysis by Christopher B. Leinberger of Robert Charles Lesser and Company, homes then were selling for $139 per square foot, 33 percent more than comparable homes in the competitive market area. Approximately 35 homes are sold each year at an average price of $335,000. Prairie Crossing has an estimated 14 percent value ratio premium over the competition. This premium, according to the market analysis, is attributed, in part, to the project's high level of amenities, its conservation ethic, and its open space.

Smart Growth Characteristics

Conservation Design
Clustering the homes at Prairie Crossing preserves the majority of the community's land as open space. Prairie Crossing's residential lots tend to be smaller than those of conventional subdivisions, which allows more lots to be developed on less land.

Environmental Features
Prairie Crossing's environmental features range from the development of wetlands and natural swale systems to the use of energy-efficient construction techniques and materials. One of the site's most unusual environmental features is its stormwater treatment system, in which swales with native plants, restored native prairies, and created wetlands and lakes serve as a sequential state-of-the-art stormwater management system. Each step in the system works to reduce the volume of runoff and increase lag time, allowing greater water infiltration and evaporation, as well as the removal of pollutants. Streets that are eight to 12 feet narrower than typical suburban residential subdivision streets further reduce runoff. By reducing street widths and using a natural stormwater drainage system, Prairie Crossing has saved more $1 million on infrastructure.

Prairie Holdings Corporation also is committed to preserving the quality of the region's open space. In coordination with the Liberty Prairie Conservancy and

Liberty Prairie Foundation, Prairie Holdings Corporation has supported volunteers and provided funding for the stewardship of the Liberty Prairie Reserve. A one-half of one percent assessment on each home sale and resale at Prairie Crossing underwrites land stewardship and other environmental projects.

Environmentally sensitive building practices that result in the reduction of energy use are employed in the 15 housing plans offered in the community. The housing plans were the first in the nation to adopt the U.S. Department of Energy's Building America program for energy-efficiency and environmental program.

Pedestrian-Oriented Design

Prairie Crossing mixes conservation design techniques with characteristics of traditional neighborhood development, combining pedestrian-oriented features that are commonly associated with both design approaches. For instance, the community's ten-mile trail system, which connects to preserved lands beyond its boundaries, can be attributed to its conservation design. Its village sidewalk system and green, and pocket parks, on the other hand, are common features of a

The community's state-of-the-art stormwater treatment system uses swales and native plants, restored native prairies, and created wetlands and lakes to protect water quality.

traditional neighborhood development. Regardless of the design influence, the result is a community that provides a variety of pedestrian-friendly opportunities.

Smart Growth Challenges

Regulatory Barriers

Prairie Crossing's stormwater drainage system called for the creation of prairies, wetlands, a lake, and drainage swales as opposed to the typical underground piping of stormwater. Initially, this approach was met with considerable skepticism from the village engineers. The owners and consultant team overcame this skepticism by demonstrating how this approach was being used successfully in other projects.

Clustering single-family homes on smaller lots was also atypical in suburban real estate developments at the time of Prairie Crossing's inception. While these home-sites embraced excellent views, the small lot sizes met resistance from the approving bodies. Other approaches encountering resistance were the community's narrow street widths and rights-of-way. While a typical Grayslake street might have 27 feet of pavement (with curb and gutter) on a 66- to 100-foot right-of-way, Prairie Crossing's 20- to 31-foot-wide pavements on 40- to 60-foot rights-of-way minimize their impact on the environment and protect more open space.

New energy-efficient building techniques did not comply with Lake County building codes. Prairie Crossing consultants, partly funded by the U.S. Department of Energy, helped to persuade county building officials to institute a voluntary alternative code, now available to any interested developer.

Untested Market

A generic obstacle to sales for the project's first two years was skepticism on the part of some potential purchasers that what Prairie Crossing was offering actually would be delivered. Expedited construction of common amenities, including the community center as well as the lake, beach, trails, stables, and tennis courts, served to dispel this skepticism.

Lessons Learned

⊙ Prairie Crossing demonstrates that conservation development is well received in the marketplace and can be financially profitable.

⊙ First-rate, upfront planning is critical to achieving reduced infrastructure costs, expediting the government approval process, and avoiding the problems characteristic of any first-time project.

⊙ According to figures compiled by Prairie Crossing financial consultant Daniel Shepard of Gleeson, Sklar, Sawyers & Cumpata, the project will generate an approximately 4.8 percent net profit return as a percentage of gross revenue. By Shepard's analysis, this return would have been 8 to 9 percent when adjusted for first-time project expenses and the unusual debt-equity financing structure of the project.

Project Data

Land Uses (Existing and Proposed)

Site size	677 acres
Residential	362 single-family houses
	(1,140 to 3,428 square feet)
Average annual sales	$14,400,000
Retail	NA (still in planning stage)
Open space	350 acres

Development Costs

Site acquisition and improvement costs	$38,100,000
Construction costs	$66,400,000
Indirect costs and financing	$32,500,000
Total	$137,000,000

Development Schedule

Site purchased	1987
Construction started	1994
Phase I completed	1999
Buildout (projected)	2004

Information Contact

Victoria Post Ranney
Prairie Crossing
32400 North Harris Road
Grayslake, Illinois 60030
847-548-4062
Fax: 847-548-4063
E-mail: vranney@aol.com
www.prairiecrossing.com

CASE STUDY: The Promenade at Westlake
Thousand Oaks, California

Smart Growth Characteristics

⊙ Collaborative planning

⊙ Pedestrian-oriented design

Smart Growth Challenge

⊙ Public opposition

The Promenade at Westlake features highly articulated storefronts that give this suburban shopping center the character of a traditional city street.

The Project

The Promenade at Westlake is a 210,000-square-foot community shopping center designed to resemble a traditional downtown. Creating a place where people want to *be,* rather than just shop, was central to this project's development philosophy. Every detail, from the selection of tenants to the design of building facades, is intended to foster a sense of place and to establish a new social destination for the affluent residents of Thousand Oaks. In the words of developer Rick Caruso, president of Caruso Affiliated Holdings (CAH), the goal of the Promenade was nothing less than "to create the center of town."

Like a traditional downtown, the Promenade has a variety of tenants that generate activity throughout the day and evening, from shops serving local needs, like a drycleaners, to entertainment-oriented retailers, including restaurants, cafés, a bookstore, a cinema, and a Club Disney for children. The town center's spaces and structures are highly articulated. Each tenant's space, whether large or small, has a characteristic design, and the bulk of the mall has been broken up into a series of smaller, visually interesting "buildings," which look as if they were built over time. The site includes a variety of outdoor spaces for sitting, dining, and strolling. The intention, according to Caruso, was to "reverse" the process of development. Instead of building a place to shop, Caruso wanted to "create a place that people want to go to," with the assumption that visitors then would stay to shop.

Several indicators have proven this entertainment theory of retailing correct at the Promenade: retail sales have averaged $450 per square foot and provisions for percentage rents came into play after just one year of operation. Behind these statistics is another barometer of success: on average, people spend four to five hours per visit at the Promenade, and many travel from beyond the expected trade area for a project of this size. The city of Thousand Oaks was so pleased with the design of the project that it is using the Promenade as the design standard for adjacent and future projects.

Smart Growth Characteristics

Collaborative Planning

Investing time and energy with the community was an essential component of the developer's success. Caruso's strategy to get the community involved and to gain their support was simple: "Give the residents what they want." The developer met with the presidents of some ten different homeowners associations and "sat with a blank piece of paper," taking notes on what residents did and did not want. For the most part, Caruso was able to deliver what the residents asked for: a bookstore, cafés, a gourmet food store, and a low-rise design built with traditional materials. On the other hand, Caruso explained what accommodations he could not make: the parking, for example, could not be hidden from view.

To further gain local residents' support, and to effectively market the project to city officials and potential tenants, the developer used an animated computer model of the project. The La Jolla Group Interactive (a southern California interactive multimedia firm), in cooperation with the Ayres Group of San Diego (a company known for its leading-edge animation techniques), developed a virtual reality "walkthrough" of the project. This presentation showed the Promenade rendered in full detail; viewers saw it as if they were actually strolling past the storefronts, courtyards, and fountains. This allowed for a particularly informed discussion of signage, heights, views, traffic, and access.

At the city council hearing for the project, each council member viewed the presentation on an individual monitor, while the audience viewed it on a ten-foot projection screen. (The presentation also aired on local cable television.) As a result of the community involvement process, the project won strong support from area residents and unanimously passed both the planning commission's and city council's reviews, a first for Thousand Oaks.

Pedestrian-Oriented Design

The Promenade's pedestrian orientation starts with two main blocks of shops with a landscaped watercourse between them. This breezeway-like space, with a fountain at the sidewalk, is used for outdoor dining for the adjacent restaurants and doubles as a pleasant passageway to a rear parking section. Fountains, each with a bronze sculpture or other feature and special-effects lighting, also are located at other focal points throughout the site.

The 15- to 20-foot-wide sidewalk—the promenade—in front of the main retail areas is paved with a variety of colored and stamped concrete and natural stone pavers, echoing and reinforcing the individuality of the various storefronts. Bollards, trees, stone flowerpots, and custom-designed pole lighting add to the mix of textures, and carts and kiosks help provide retail energy and interest along the route.

Smart Growth Challenge

Public Opposition

The 22.5-acre Promenade parcel was known locally as a difficult site; two other developers had tried and failed to develop the property before CAH acquired it. Though the site had good freeway access, excellent demographics, and no serious limitations, it was not considered to be in a retail area, and neighborhood residents had objected to earlier attempts to develop it.

Knowing this—and because of it—Caruso considered it an ideal site; he believes that prior, unsuccessful development attempts "create a road map for you." Moreover, notes Caruso, a slow-growth or antigrowth environment "by nature creates a barrier to entry of competition" and usually means the area is underserved. Using the community involvement techniques cited above helped Caruso to gain the support of local residents and public officials, while also attracting retailers to the shopping center.

Lessons Learned

⊙ Community participation during the planning and design phases is essential in obtaining support for a project, particularly in a slow-growth or antigrowth environment.

⊙ With its high-quality design and detailing, pedestrian-friendly environment, and entertainment-focused leasing strategy, the Promenade has shown that the standard community shopping center can attract many types of activities throughout the day.

⊙ While it may not be a town center in the historical sense, the social and environmental features the Promenade has drawn from the traditional town center model represent a promising direction for community shopping center development.

Project Data

Land Uses

Site area	22.5 acres
Gross building area (GBA)	210,000 square feet
Gross leasable area (GLA)	201,572 square feet
Floor/area ratio	0.214
Parking	1,296 surface spaces

Land Use Plan

Use	Acres	Percent of Site
Buildings	5	22%
Paved area[1]	10	45%
Landscaped area	3	13%
Dedicated space[2]	4.5	20%
Total	22.5	100%

[1]Surface parking and roads.
[2]Arroyo.

Retail Data

Length of leases	5–25 years
Annual rents	$24–$72 per square foot
Average annual sales	$450 per square foot

Development Costs

Site acquisition cost	$12,465,786
Site improvement cost	$ 8,427,615
Construction costs	$10,553,178
Soft costs	$10,192,641
Total	$41,639,220

Development Schedule

Planning started	August 1995
Leasing started	August 1995
Site purchased	December 1995
Approvals obtained	January 1996
Construction started	February 1996
Project opened	November 1996

Information Contact

Caruso Affiliated Holdings
100 Wilshire Boulevard, 14th Floor
Santa Monica, California 90401
310-458-0202

CASE STUDY: Rancho Santa Margarita
Rancho Santa Margarita, California

Smart Growth Characteristics

⊙ Master-planned community

⊙ Open space protection/environmental features

⊙ Mixed-use development

Smart Growth Challenge

⊙ Regulatory barriers

A system of pedestrian and bicycle trails runs throughout Rancho Santa Margarita.

The Project

Although conceived in the early 1980s, the master-planned community of Rancho Santa Margarita incorporates many of the principles that smart growth advocates today. Located in southeast Orange County, California, this community of nearly 40,000 residents rests on 5,000 acres, of which 50 percent is protected open space. Like other well-planned communities, Rancho Santa Margarita includes a mix of housing, commercial, and retail development. A town center serves as the community's central gathering place and the location of many of its retail stores. An elaborate system of pedestrian trails and neighborhood parks offers residents numerous alternatives to driving, as well as a variety of recreational opportunities. The community's mixed-use design reduces the total number and length of automobile trips, since many residents also work and shop in Rancho Santa Margarita.

The community also provides affordable housing for Orange County residents. Rancho Santa Margarita's housing options include apartments, townhomes, and single-family houses, which range in cost from about $150,000 to $300,000. The gross density of its initial village is ten units per acre; specific development products have achieved densities of more than 25 units per acre. Sixty-five percent of the units meet the county's affordable housing criteria. The community accommodates a significant portion of the region's dynamic growth. Perhaps most importantly, Rancho Santa Margarita has proven to be very successful in the marketplace. Its annualized absorption rate since it opened in 1986 ranks near the top for master-planned communities nationwide.

Smart Growth Characteristics

Master-Planned Community

Rancho Santa Margarita is a 5,000-acre new community that has been phased in over a 14-year period. It is located adjacent to existing development, thus allowing for efficient extension of infrastructure. Developed in essentially five phases—Rancho Trabuco, EastLake, the Town Center, the Business Park, and Golf Village—Rancho Santa Margarita was designed to preserve natural systems, mix land uses, and create a unique identity or "sense of place." The master-planned community was designed at three levels, the largest of which was the community level, followed by the village and the neighborhood levels. Detailed planning was conducted at each of these levels to ensure a consistent community character and an appropriate integration of land uses. A town center provides a central place for residents to congregate, shop, and recreate.

Open Space Protection/Environmental Features

Rancho Santa Margarita's developers have preserved significant natural resources by dedicating 50 percent of the site to community open space. This open space contribution protects sensitive habitat, thus offsetting the higher-density nature of the community. In addition to protecting natural resource areas, the community's designers paid a tremendous amount of attention to the community's public spaces. These places, which include public parks, town center plazas, and pedestrian and bicycle trails, contribute to the everyday experiences of those who live, work, and play in the community. The trails also provide a transportation choice for community residents and employees.

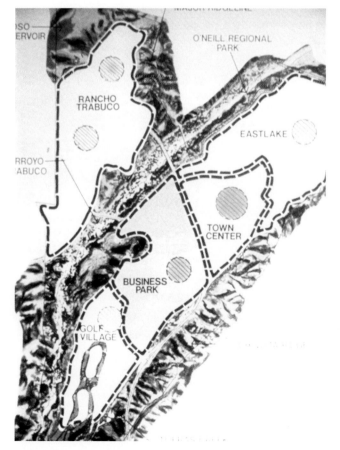

Rancho Santa Margarita is a 5,000-acre multi-phased, comprehensively planned community.

Mixed-Use Development

The scale and design of Rancho Santa Margarita provided opportunities to put in place a mix of land uses and a variety of housing types. By integrating jobs, shopping, and housing, the community is able to balance jobs and housing and, in turn, reduce the length and frequency of automobile trips. Rancho Santa Margarita's developers also point out that creating a jobs/housing balance enabled them to build fewer roads, accelerate housing absorption, and add to the overall economic base of the community. Also contributing to the success of Rancho Santa Margarita is its 250-acre town center, which includes a pedestrian plaza and main street, and serves as the community's central gathering place. The variety of housing that Rancho Santa Margarita offers—including garden apartments, condominiums, townhouses, detached bungalows, and larger single-family houses—is another important element of its success. The community's higher-density housing helped maximize absorption and raise residual values. The result is a housing stock of more than 13,000 units that serves a mix of incomes and provides housing for people in all stages of life.

Smart Growth Challenge

Regulatory Barriers

Rancho Santa Margarita's wide streets are a result of local development regulations. The street system thus is scaled more to the automobile than to the pedestrian. While an extensive system of pedestrian trails services the community well, the road widths and subsequent automobile activity detract from the community's original design objective of creating an ideal pedestrian-oriented community.

Lesson Learned

⊙ While Rancho Santa Margarita achieves numerous smart growth principles, the community could have incorporated more diversity in its architecture and could have attempted to provide smaller increments of retail development in its neighborhoods, according to Steve Kellenberg, principal, EDAW, Inc.

Project Data

Site area	5,000 acres
Gross residential density	5.6 (does not include the 2,500 acres of open space.)

Land Use Plan

Use	Acres
Residential	1,620
Commercial	94
Industrial	131
Office	88
Other (including plazas, parking, trails, golf course)	485
Total developed land	2,418
Undeveloped land	2,582

Dwelling Unit Data

Type	Number
Single-family detached	5,192
Attached	8,096
Total	13,288

Employees

Type	Number
Commercial	2,789
Industrial	4,403
Office	5,208
Other	525
Total	12,925

Information Contact

Steve Kellenberg
Principal
EDAW, Inc.
17875 Von Karman Avenue
Suite 400
Irvine, California 92614
949-660-8044

CASE STUDY: Reston Town Center
Reston, Virginia

Smart Growth Characteristics

⊙ Town center

⊙ Traditional neighborhood design

Smart Growth Challenges

⊙ Regulatory barriers

⊙ Untested market

Reston Town Center has distinguished itself as a vibrant place to live, work, and play. It is as active in the evening as it is during the business day.

The Project

Reston Town Center is considered the heart of one of the most prominent master-planned communities in the United States. As a result of its urban ambience, the project has become a 24-hour central gathering place—a civic center where people go to see a movie, dine in a restaurant, or enjoy a community event in the central plaza.

The community of Reston is the product of Robert E. Simon, Jr.'s vision for an alternative to conventional suburban development. Its development began in 1963 on 7,400 acres of land 18 miles southwest of Washington, D.C., in Fairfax County, Virginia. Reston is now home to nearly 100,000 residents, 3,500 businesses, and almost 50,000 employees.

The town center is an 85-acre component of a larger 460-acre mixed-use district identified in Reston's original 1962 master plan. The first phase of the town center, Fountain Square, includes 530,000 square feet of office space; 240,000 square feet of retail, restaurant, and entertainment space; and a 514-room Hyatt Regency Hotel. The centerpiece of Fountain Square is an open-air civic plaza featuring a large fountain, outdoor seating, artwork, and—in the winter—an ice-skating rink.

The development of Phases II and III, known as Freedom Square and Explorer Square, respectively, began in 1998 with the construction of One Freedom Square, an 18-story, 400,000-square-foot office and retail building. These phases will add to Reston Town Center's urban experience by providing additional street-level retail and more office space. Together, Phases II and III will consist of 1,560,000 square feet of

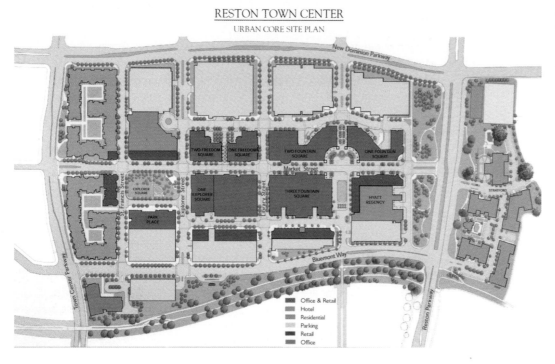

RESTON TOWN CENTER
URBAN CORE SITE PLAN

office space, 250,000 square feet of retail space, another premier 500-room hotel, 700 residential units, six acres of open space, and a four-acre park.

The residential components, which are being codeveloped by Reston-based Terrabrook and Atlanta-based Trammell Crow Residential, include Stratford at Reston Town Center, a 334-unit condominium community that has been under development since 1998. A second residential neighborhood at Explorer Square will feature 700 luxury rental apartments. Altogether, at buildout, Reston Town Center will contain 1,034 residential units.

Unlike many other business centers, Reston Town Center has distinguished itself as a vibrant place to live, work, and play. It is as active in the evening as it is during the business day. Reminiscent of the Main Street of days gone by, Reston Town Center has become a regional destination for people looking to shop, eat, or spend leisure time.

Smart Growth Characteristics

Town Center

In 1981, recognizing that the Reston community soon would be large enough to support its own downtown, Reston Land Corporation (RLC)—a subsidiary of Mobil Land Development Corporation and Reston's master developer from 1978 through 1996—initiated detailed planning for an 85-acre mixed-use district that would act as the community's urban core.

The first section of Reston Town Center, occupying 20 acres on the eastern end of the 85-acre urban core, opened in 1990. The mixed-use project includes twin 11-story office buildings; a 514-room Hyatt Regency hotel with extensive conference facilities and an executive fitness center; street-level retail, restaurants, and entertainment uses with professional offices above; and surface and structured parking for more than 3,000 cars.

Terrabrook bought the future sections of Reston Town Center from RLC in 1996 and has been the master developer since that time. One Freedom Square, the first of six office towers in Phase II, was completed in fall 1999 and is home to Andersen Consulting (Accenture, as of January 1, 2001) and the prestigious law firms of Cooley Godward and Hale & Door. The 400,000-square-foot building is one of Reston's most visible new landmarks.

As part of the approval process for Reston Town Center, RLC negotiated a shared-parking agreement with the local government to recognize the efficiencies of the mixed-use project, thereby reducing the parking requirement for the first section from 4,100 to 3,100 spaces. A transportation association, known as LINK, also was formed to educate the public about transportation alternatives, refine regional transit systems routing to the development, and advocate various demand-reduction strategies.

Traditional Neighborhood Design

The plan for Reston Town Center intentionally incorporated positive characteristics of both urban and suburban development—pedestrian-scaled streets, a variety of land uses and services, open spaces, easy vehicular access, and ample parking. Custom-designed paving and benches complement the architecture and reinforce the human-scale comfort and accessibility. Large trees and seasonal planting beds give the streets and plazas a sense of liveliness and maturity. Streets and sidewalks are proportioned to balance spaciousness and ease of movement with an intimate, human scale. The sidewalks are wider on the sunny side of the street and the roadway is narrow so that pedestrians are encouraged to cross from one side of the street to another.

Reston Town Center's developers realized that a variety of retail storefronts would help to create a vibrant pedestrian experience. Its buildings were designed to accommodate a continuum of storefronts at the ground level of every building, with variations in setbacks, entrances, awnings, bay windows, and signage to produce a recurring sense of surprise and the impression that the town has evolved over time.

Reston Town Center has become a central gathering place for residents of Reston and surrounding communities. Creating a sense of place by providing innovative, attractive community amenities was central to achieving that goal. The first of these amenities, the 5,400-square-foot pavilion in Fountain Square, is the setting for community concerts during the summer and ice skating in the winter. Terrabrook will build the second, a 4,000-square-foot enclosed art gallery, in a future development phase.

FIVE PRINCIPLES IN PLANNING RESTON TOWN CENTER

1) The town center had to be walkable; its core had to be 100 acres or less.

2) The town center had to contain a mix of uses—office, retail, restaurants, entertainment, and residential.

3) These uses had to be dense enough to bring a critical mass of people (workers, shoppers, residents) into the town center.

4) The spaces had to be attractive enough that people would choose to go to the town center.

5) The town center had to be easily accessible by car and by transit.

These planning principles have assisted the Reston Town Center in differentiating it from other business centers and have created a sense of place that both employers and residents want to be.

Smart Growth Challenges

Regulatory Barriers

The project required rezoning from Fairfax County. The rezoning process began in 1984, took approximately three years, and involved several revised submissions. RLC's initial rezoning request for the 460-acre Town Center District was for rights to develop 8.4 million square feet of commercial space and at least 1,400 residential units.

The predominant issue was traffic. Negotiations led to the creation of a performance rezoning for a minimum of 6.8 million square feet of commercial space, including 5.5 million square feet of office space, and 1,400 residential units. Up to 1.6 million square feet of additional office space will be permitted if traffic forecasts prove to be accurate and if the project meets the developers trip-generation objectives. Transportation "proffers" (developer-funded and -implemented improvements), including pavement and rights-of-way, are valued at $45 million for the program being implemented.

Untested Market

The county initially was concerned that Reston Town Center's retail and residential components were too small and that the residential component was not sufficiently integrated with the commercial development. RLC committed to expanding the retail component (thereby reducing office and/or hotel components) if demand proved sufficient. RLC also argued that since Reston already had a strong and diverse residential base, the town center did not need to be self sufficient. The county and RLC agreed to defer residential building in the remaining portions of the town center district until after the amenities necessary to support an urban lifestyle were in place.

A maximum of 3,465,000 square feet of development is permitted in the 85-acre Town Center District. This includes 2.15 million square feet of office space, 315,000 square feet of retail space, and 1 million square feet of hotel space. The maximum floor/area ratio for the site is therefore 0.94; there is no density limit on specific parcels.

Timing is critical for a major mixed-use center. The density and mix of Reston Town Center's first phase required the critical mass of population, employment, and income that Reston and the surrounding area had achieved by the late 1980s.

Lessons Learned

⊙ It is important to define a project's market niche carefully and prepare a development plan accordingly.

⊙ Market demand for space in a well-planned mixed-use development is greater than space in a comparable single-use development.

⊙ Entertainment uses, as well as programmed cultural and recreational events, are a crucial component for making a town center a vibrant place.

Project Data

Land Use Plan

(in square feet, unless otherwise noted)

Use	Existing	Proposed	Total
Residential	334 units	700 units	1,034 units
Office	930,000	1.16 million	2.1 million
Hotel	514 rooms	500 rooms	1,014 rooms
Retail	240,000	250,000	490,000
Open space	–	6 acres	6 acres
Civic/cultural space	5,400	4,000	9,400

Development Costs

(in millions of dollars)

Type	Existing	Proposed (estimated)	Total
Site acquisition cost	$30	$58	$88
Site improvement cost	$15	$4	$19
Construction costs	$189	$292	$481
Soft costs	$79	$58	$137
Total	$313	$412	$725

Other Data

Average annual retail net rent	$25 per square foot
Average annual retail net rent (including percentage rent)	$35 per square foot
Average length of retail tenant lease	Five years
Average office tenant size (30 tenants)	9,397 square feet
Average annual office rents Approximately	$23 to $27 per square foot
Average length of lease (retail and office)	Three to five years

Development Schedule

Phase I grand opening	1990
Phase II construction began	1998
Buildout (expected)	2004

Information Contact

Terrabrook
11450 Baron Cameron Avenue
Reston, Virginia 20190
703-787-7500

PART FOUR

Resource Guide

This resource guide is a collection of various tools that can be helpful in developing and implementing a smart growth program. It includes a step-by-step program (and corresponding sample agendas) to assist organizations and individuals in starting a smart growth program. The guide also contains detailed descriptions of specific elements of the smart growth programs in Austin, Texas (the city's smart growth matrix); Maryland (the state's building rehabilitation code program); and Silicon Valley, California (the Housing Action Coalition of Santa Clara County's Project Endorsement Program). The resource guide concludes with some tips on working with the media, a list of organizations that provide smart growth information, and a ULI smart growth resources page.

Getting Started: A Step-by-Step Smart Growth Program

ULI–the Urban Land Institute's national smart growth program was established to promote best practice examples and bring together stakeholders with various interests. Serving as the "tent" under which diverse groups can gather, ULI's smart growth program demonstrates that collaborative processes can build a better understanding and trust between traditionally divergent interests that can lead to a shared set of solutions. Using a collaborative national model as a prototype, the Institute's local and regional forums and programs, often led by ULI District Councils, identify solutions most appropriate to the unique economic, environmental, and cultural landscapes of participating communities. Through it all, a set of steps needed to initiate a smart growth program has been established. Those steps are as follows:

Identify Leadership

Identifying a leader or set of leaders who are willing to "own" the process is central to the success of any smart growth initiative. These leaders should be objective and well respected in the community. They should be intensely interested in the future of the region (and in land use issues in general), and should have a desire to work toward a commonly shared set of goals. ULI's experiences show that leadership has been essential to the smart growth efforts taking place in Atlanta; Washington, D.C.; Chicago; and Charlotte.

Compile Information on Demographic, Economic, and Environmental Trends

Many of the challenges that smart growth seeks to address, such as traffic congestion and the loss of open space, can be highly charged, with individuals or groups of stakeholders strongly committed to conflicting viewpoints. In such an environment, it is especially important to understand the economic, demographic, and environmental trends that are driving these challenges in the region. This information can serve as the baseline around which a productive discussion can take place and can help diffuse no-growth versus progrowth perspectives. An understanding of these trends can shine light on specific challenges that should be evaluated in a smart growth program. Those gathering this information should ensure that it comes from reliable, unbiased sources. Regional councils of governments and local universities are good information sources.

Identify Key Stakeholder Groups

Identifying representatives of key stakeholder groups from throughout the region may be the most important step in initiating a smart growth program. Stakeholder groups that should be represented include the development and real estate communities, the public sector, the academic community, environmental and civic organizations, and other business and industry groups. A smart growth program that excludes these stakeholders runs the risk of being labeled a biased initiative. Those seeking representatives from these key groups should ask leaders from each of the targeted interest groups for their help in the identification process, to ensure that the most appropriate participants are identified and that the smart growth process is a truly collaborative one. Successful smart growth programs, such as those highlighted here, encourage all voices to be heard. In the end, solutions developed by a broad range of stakeholders will be supported by a broad range of stakeholders, thus improving the likelihood of their successful implementation.

Involve Stakeholders, Seek Common Ground

Once the leadership is in place, information has been gathered, and a core set of stakeholders has been identified, the next step is to convene a series of meetings and/or forums. While numerous approaches to organizing meetings and working toward common solutions exist, ULI has found that facilitated roundtable discussions are a good way to get all stakeholders to begin to participate in the process. (Sample agendas for the two types of programs described below follow this section of the "Resource Guide.")

A smart growth leadership issues forum (with 25 to 35 participants) can help get local and regional leaders involved in the smart growth process. Beginning the forum with a presentation on community trends will set the stage for the facilitated discussion that follows. This type of roundtable discussion can build trust between historically divergent viewpoints, identify common ground as well as barriers to smart growth, and set the stage for future events. Starting the program by spelling out some specific roundtable objectives and ending with some specific action items will keep these leaders involved and interested.

After these initial roundtable discussions have been held and some common areas of agreement have been identified, the next step should be to reach out to a larger audience, to solicit their input and buy-in. This can be done through a regional roundtable or symposium format (with 150 to 300 attendees). Technology-based techniques, including electronic voting and growth and development simulation technologies, increasingly are used to broaden the input and buy-in into smart growth issues. Again, the broader the support for a set of solutions, the more likely they are to be advanced.

Develop an Action Plan, Begin Implementation, and Monitor Progress

After stakeholders have been convened and some common ground forged, an action plan that outlines specific implementation activities should be developed, in coordination with the core stakeholder group to ensure that the plan is consistent with past agreements. Once such a plan is put into place, each of the stakeholder groups should use its own organization to support the plan's implementation. These groups can dedicate staff and/or other resources or seek outside funding to advance the action plan. As the plan is implemented, its progress should be monitored and periodically reported on to the core stakeholder groups and to a broader audience. Developing benchmarks that measure the success of the action plan's implementation is one way to monitor and report on its progress.

These steps should assist stakeholders in pursuing a collaborative smart growth program. While exactly how the steps are implemented will vary according to the unique characteristics of each community, these generic steps can guide local smart growth programs on the road to success.

Sample Smart Growth Meeting Agendas

Smart Growth Leadership Issues Forum Agenda

(Intended for 25 to 50 participants)

Desired Forum Outcomes:

1) Establish open lines of communication among various stakeholders as a basis for a continuing process.

2) Develop a common vision for the region that draws on earlier efforts.

3) Identify economic, environmental, and social goals to achieve this vision.

4) Identify the challenges and impediments to achieving the common vision.

5) List the next steps and actions necessary to move the process forward.

Agenda

7:30 a.m.
Continental Breakfast

8:00 a.m.
Welcome/Overview
Prominent leaders from the business and environmental communities are good prospects to cochair the forum. Their leadership can set the tone for an open discussion and ensure that all perspectives and views are heard during the course of the day.

8:15 a.m.
Trends Presentation: Demographic, Economic, and Environmental Trends
Providing a balanced report on regional trends (job, housing, and population growth; water and air quality) can set the stage for the day's deliberations. A well-respected and unbiased academic often is the best person to present this information.

9:00 a.m.
Articulate a Vision for the Region: What Does the Future Look Like?
A well-facilitated visioning discussion achieves two of the forum's goals. First, it can get all participants involved in the discussion. (In fact, the facilitator should ask each participant to present his or her vision for the region.) Second, it demonstrates the considerable overlap of ideas that environmentalists, business leaders, and others have for the region. This helps to establish open lines of communication among participants.

10:00 a.m.
Break
(The remainder of the meeting is facilitated.)

10:15 a.m.
Smart Growth Issue #1
[A key issue of importance to the region, such as land use, transportation, housing, the environment, or social equity, can be discussed.]

Opening comments by:
* *A representative of an environmental or civic organization;*
* *A representative of the business/development sector; and*
* *A representative of the public sector.*

Discussion questions:

1) From your point of view, what are the "Issue #1" goals needed to accommo-date future growth in the metropolitan region?

2) What steps might leaders in the region take to address these goals?

3) What current policies/examples best reflect your vision?

4) What impediments exist to accomplishing your vision?

11:15 a.m.
Smart Growth Issue #2
[A second issue that is key to the region can be addressed.]

Opening comments by:
- *A representative of an environmental or civic organization;*
- *A representative of the business/development sector; and*
- *A representative of the public sector.*

Discussion questions:

1) From your point of view, what are the "Issue #2" goals needed to accommo-date future growth in the metropolitan region?

2) What steps might leaders in the region take to address these goals?

3) What current policies/examples best reflect your vision?

4) What impediments exist to accomplishing your vision?

12:15 p.m.
Lunch and Case Study Presentation
A case study on a successful smart growth initiative might be presented during lunch. The case study should be selected on the basis of its transferability to the region. (ULI smart growth forums have presented smart growth initiatives in Maryland, Pennsylvania, Georgia, Utah, Austin, and Silicon Valley.)

1:15 p.m.
Roundtable Discussions
Participants break out into assigned groups to discuss topical questions in depth. (These questions may be refined as a result of the morning's discussion.) Suggested questions:

1) What environmental priorities are needed to achieve a healthy regional ecosys-tem and a high quality of life?

2) How can we achieve a mix of land uses that ensures an efficient use of both the region's transportation system and its land?

3) How can we encourage affordable housing near employment sites throughout the region?

4) What opportunities exist for creating a regional open space network?

5) How do we address the barriers to and increase public acceptance of high-density development where it the most efficient use of land and infrastructure?

2:15 p.m.
Report Out: Plenary Discussion
Participants reconvene to discuss key findings from each of the roundtables. A representative from each group presents the group's top three goals, challenges, resources, and next steps.

2:45 p.m.
Recap and Next Steps
The forum cochairs can close the session by building a list of concrete action items that can be taken to advance the smart growth effort.

3:00 p.m.
Adjourn

Smart Growth Regional Symposium Agenda

(Intended for 150 to 300 attendees)

7:45 a.m.
Continental Breakfast

8:15 a.m.
Welcome and Symposium Overview
Cochairs from different interests—such as development, environment, civic, and business interests—lead the symposium.

8:30 a.m.
Trends Presentation: Demographic, Economic, and Environmental Trends
Providing a balanced report on the trends in a region (job, housing, and population growth; water and air quality) can set the stage for the day's deliberations. A well-respected and unbiased academic often is the best person to present this information.

9:30 a.m.
Articulating Smart Growth Principles
During facilitated roundtable discussions, conference participants discuss principles that can help guide a region's future. This discussion will ensure that all attendees have an opportunity to play an active role in the symposium.

10:15 a.m.
Break

10:30 a.m.
Exploring Challenges and Solutions to Implementing Smart Growth Principles
Successful projects and policies that reflect the principles of smart growth exist in every region. Successful projects can be presented in concurrent break-out sessions. Each presentation might highlight what impediments were faced, how they were overcome, and how the successes might be replicated. Case studies to be examined could include:

1) A mixed-use suburban development project;
2) A transit-oriented development project;
3) An urban infill or redevelopment project; and/or
4) A public/private partnership initiative.

12:00 p.m.
Lunch and Case Study Presentation
Another case study of a successful smart growth initiative can be presented during lunch. The case study should be selected on the basis of its transferability to the region. (ULI smart growth forums have presented smart growth initiatives in Maryland, Pennsylvania, Georgia, Utah, Austin, and Silicon Valley.)

1:45 p.m.
Next Steps for the Region
During a moderated plenary panel, representatives of the business, public, environmental, and civic communities discuss what they learned and what next steps should be taken to advance the concepts that were explored throughout the day.

3:00 p.m.
Wrap-Up and Concluding Remarks

Sample Smart Growth Programs

Austin, Texas's Smart Growth Matrix

Overview

The smart growth matrix is a tool to assist the city council in analyzing development proposals within the Desired Development Zone. It is designed to measure how well a development project meets the city's smart growth goals, including the location of development, proximity to mass transit, urban design characteristics, compliance with nearby neighborhood plans, increases in the tax base, and other policy priorities.

If a development project, as measured by the matrix, significantly advances the city's goals, financial incentives may be available to help offset the high cost of developing in urban areas. These incentives may include waiver of development fees and public investment in new or improved infrastructure such as water and sewer lines, streets or streetscape improvements, or similar facilities. Incentives available under the smart growth matrix require city council review and approval.

Summary of the Process

Stage 1: Preliminary Review. The applicant begins by contacting city staff to obtain a smart growth matrix application packet. The applicant then evaluates the project using the matrix and schedules a meeting with the staff review team to present details of the project. After the initial meeting, city staff conduct a preliminary matrix review of the project to provide an assessment of how it meets the city's smart growth goals and present a preliminary score to the applicant.

Stage 2: Formal Review. Upon receipt of site plan approval, the applicant submits the matrix application with support materials to the city's department of planning, environmental, and conservation services for formal review. The city review team then formally scores the project and estimates the value of potential incentives.

Stage 3: Contract. City staff present the proposed incentives to the city council for review and approval. After approval by the city council, the applicant and city staff negotiate a contract to implement an incentive package.

Stage 4: Permits/Construction. City staff process fee waivers and reimburse fees already paid by the applicant. City staff also monitor the project during construction to ensure that the contract is fulfilled.

Smart Growth Matrix Scoring System and Incentive Levels

A maximum point value is assigned to each of the criteria in the matrix. The final score for each project is dependent on how many of the criteria the project meets. There are four point levels, three of which may qualify a project for incentives. Projects receiving 0 to 225 points are not eligible for any incentives. Those receiving 226 to 300 points may qualify for waiver of 50 percent of applicable city fees. Projects that score between 301 and 375 points may qualify for waiver of 100 percent of applicable city fees, plus city participation in certain infrastructure improvements. (The total value of all incentives cannot exceed the net present value of the increase in property tax revenues generated by the project over five years; see examples below.) Finally, projects that score 376 to 635 points may qualify for waiver of 100 percent of applicable city fees and city participation in certain infrastructure improvements. (The total value of these incentives cannot exceed the net present value of the increase in property tax revenues generated by the project over ten years; see examples below.)

For projects that score in the two highest levels (301 points or more) the maximum value of potential incentives is tied to the increased property taxes generated by the new project. This is calculated as follows:

⊙ Multiply the estimated appraised value of the project by the current city tax rate to obtain the annual increase in property taxes.

⊙ Multiply this annual increase in property taxes by either five or ten years, depending on the points that the project received, to obtain the total increase in property taxes.

⊙ The total increase in property taxes then is discounted for inflation and interest to obtain the net present value of the increase in property taxes.

Example of Calculation:

Estimated value of project at completion	$20,000,000
Less current assessed value	$(500,000)
Net increase in assessed value	$15,500,000
Annual city property tax revenue	$100,000
Five-year net present value of property tax	$375,000 revenue
Ten-year net present value of property tax	$700,000 revenue

In this example, a project that scored between 301 and 375 points could qualify for up to $375,000 in fee waivers and infrastructure investments such as water and wastewater lines, sidewalks, or similar improvements. If the project scored between 376 and 635 points, it could qualify for up to $700,000 in fee waivers and infrastructure investments.

Maryland's Building Rehabilitation Code Program

In April 2000, the Maryland General Assembly and Governor Parris Glendening passed smart codes legislation creating the Maryland building rehabilitation code program. This program is designed to encourage investment in existing neighborhoods through the rehabilitation and reuse of existing buildings. A new component of Maryland's smart growth initiative, the program centers on the development of a new state code that will establish construction code requirements for work on existing buildings. The rehabilitation code will facilitate the rehabilitation of existing buildings in at least three ways. It will integrate the ten codes that now commonly govern construction work on existing buildings in Maryland into one document; it will clearly separate rehabilitation requirements from those for new construction; and it will set up an easy-to-use framework of code requirements that gradually increase as the scope of the rehabilitation project increases: the smaller the project, the fewer the code requirements that apply.

Why the State Needs a Building Rehabilitation Code

Professionals in the building codes and development fields repeatedly have raised concerns that the application of Maryland's current construction codes can present significant barriers to the improvement or redevelopment of existing buildings. The state currently regulates building construction with a complex patchwork of ten individual codes that vary from one local jurisdiction to another. These include a building code, fire code, mechanical code, plumbing code, electrical code, boiler safety code, energy code, elevator code, accessibility code, and provisions for historic structures. This framework of codes can pose at least four distinct barriers to redevelopment:

Lack of uniformity. The state's construction codes sometimes overlap, resulting in unclear requirements.

Unpredictability. Code requirements vary among jurisdictions and code interpretations vary among enforcement officials.

Inflexibility. Codes can be inflexibly applied to existing buildings.

Need for training. Statewide, code officials, design professionals, and building contractors need code training.

Rehabilitation Code Legislation

The legislation passed in April 2000 sets out the goals and parameters of the rehabilitation code and charges a coordinating body—the Rehabilitation Code Advisory Council, with 27 members appointed by the governor for three-year terms—with drafting the nuts and bolts of the code by December 31, 2000. The new code will be based on a model rehabilitation code developed by the U.S. Department of Housing and Urban Development (HUD) and the National Association of Home Builders (NAHB). With the advice of the advisory council, the Maryland Department of Housing and Community Development will be responsible for promulgating the provisions of the rehabilitation code through the Maryland Code of Regulations (COMAR) process.

The advisory council will coordinate the efforts of the government and private organizations that are involved in administering and working with the state's construction codes, and will act as an umbrella body with three primary functions: to draft and periodically update the rehabilitation code; to issue advisory resolutions of issues that arise in implementing the new code; and to oversee training for code officials, design professionals, and others in the construction industry.

To facilitate the statewide implementation of the rehabilitation code, the smart codes enabling legislation also requires that the state agencies responsible for regulating the building industry revisit their codes to ensure that they work in harmony with the new rehabilitation code.

Statewide Implementation

The rehabilitation code will be implemented using the current state building code, the Maryland Building Performance Standards, as a model. Under this framework, the rehabilitation code will operate statewide. Local jurisdictions can amend its provisions but, to encourage uniformity and the greatest degree of rehabilitation activity, the state will provide financial incentives for localities that choose not to amend the new code. These incentives include new money allocated above FY 2000 funding levels in the following state programs: the Maryland Department of Housing and Community Development's circuit rider rehabilitation code inspector, rehabilitation code training, and smart growth mortgage programs; the Maryland Department of Transportation's neighborhood conservation program; and the Rural Legacy Advisory Board's rural legacy program. Municipalities and counties that do not amend the rehabilitation code also will be eligible for priority funding under the transportation enhancements program administered by the Maryland Department of Transportation Advisory Council.

Rehabilitation Code Successes

Maryland is not the first state to adopt a building rehabilitation code. Just one year after New Jersey adopted a similar code in 1997, investment in rehabilitation work rose statewide by nearly 8 percent. Rehabilitation investment increased most significantly in three older communities: Newark saw a 60 percent increase (from $68 to nearly $109 million), Jersey City experienced an 83 percent increase (from $49 to almost $90 million), and Trenton saw a 40 percent increase (from $21 to $30 million). HUD also has determined that the application of a rehabilitation code similar to the code being developed for Maryland reduced the rehabilitation costs to renovate a single-family farmhouse by 15 to 20 percent.

For a copy of the working draft of Maryland's rehabilitation code, go to www.mdp.state.md.us/smartgrowth/smartcode/smartcode00.htm.

The Housing Action Coalition of Santa Clara County's Project Endorsement Program

Overview

The Housing Action Coalition is composed of a broad range of organizations and interests whose members have as a common goal—the provision of affordable, well-constructed, and appropriately located housing in Santa Clara County. The lack of relatively affordable and accessible housing continues to be a key concern of Santa Clara County residents and employers. To address this concern, the Housing Action Coalition created a project endorsement program that has helped or directly resulted in the approval of 71 housing projects, representing 24,000 new homes.

How the Endorsement Process Works

A request for support should be received at least four weeks before the action for support is needed. The Housing Action Coalition encourages developers to contact the coalition at the earliest possible date, preferably at the design development stage. This allows the project to be adequately reviewed, and time for the Housing Action Coalition to thoroughly examine the project through its committee process. The coalition may consider specific plans, master plans, and general plan amendments that would likely result in housing developments that reflect the guidelines in this statement.

Requests should include at least the following information:

Proposed development. A map of the proposal (a site plan and an area map, as well as its geographic location) should be submitted along with the following development details:

⊙ The time line for development;

⊙ The total number of units, plus the number of bedrooms per unit;

⊙ The total acreage of the development;

⊙ Elevations;

⊙ Plans for mixed uses;

⊙ The location of the nearest rail or bus transit station and information on service frequency;

⊙ Information on traffic levels of service, and a mitigation plan, if needed;

⊙ A list of interested parties, both potential supporters and opponents; and

⊙ The proposed price of units, the number of units proposed at each price level, and the range of incomes necessary to purchase or rent these properties.

Environmental review. Projects that require either an Environmental Impact Review (EIR) or an Environmental Impact Statement (EIS) should submit a draft summary of the report with their proposal. If further information is required, HAC will contact the applicant for submittal of a full report.

Political process. The person(s) or organizations submitting the request should provide a schedule of public hearings and their locations.

Background summary. A brief background summary should be included with the request for support that describes past work in the area and background information on the applicant.

Endorsement. Requests should be sent to the Housing Action Coalition.

Endorsement Criteria

Location. The project must be within an existing city urban service area. In order to maximize the compatibility with public transit and minimize automobile use, the project should be within one-half mile of major transit service or a job center, or within one-quarter mile of a town center that will provide a future focus for transit. (Major transit service is defined as a rail station or a bus stop served by six or more buses per hour in peak periods; it also includes funded, but not yet built, fixed-rail stations.) The project can be within two miles of a rail transit station if provisions are made to provide ongoing shuttle service to residents.

Density. As a general rule, the project should have an overall density of at least 14 units per acre. This minimum density does not require 14 units on each individual acre within the development; rather it is the minimum average number of units on a project's total acreage. The coalition is willing to consider projects with lower densities in jurisdictions that have a history of significantly lower densities, if the project density is significantly higher than the norm for that jurisdiction. The coalition also may recommend developments with average densities of less than 14 units per acre if warranted by site-specific conditions. For developments located within a half-mile of a rail transit station, special consideration will be given to proposals with densities of at least 20 units per acre and at the higher end of the jurisdiction's allowable range.

Affordability. The HAC seeks to promote balanced communities that provide housing for households with different needs and income levels. For this reason, it advocates new housing developments of all types, including affordable housing, market-rate housing, and mixed-income housing. The HAC strongly encourages developments that increase the supply of affordable housing in Silicon Valley. Developments that receive public financing should include a proportional affordable component.

Affordable housing shall be defined as follows: Homeless housing is housing affordable to households at or below 35 percent of the area median income. Affordable rental housing is housing that is affordable to households with incomes up to 80 percent of the area median income. Affordable ownership housing is defined as for-sale housing that is affordable to households with incomes up to 120 percent of the area median income

Design. The project should stress high-quality design and construction to help ensure its long-term contribution to the improvement of the neighborhood. The buildings should fit their setting, complementing and enhancing the existing neighborhood. The project should promote social interaction through pedestrian-friendly design, innovative parking, and other principles of urban village design. It should address transit use and access and, where appropriate, the potential for mixed uses.

Size. The project should total at least 50 units. In exceptional circumstances, smaller projects may be considered. Such circumstances could include exemplary design, an unusually high level of affordability, or multiple small compatible projects in the immediate vicinity that have the potential for creating viable neighborhoods.

Safety. In order to assure the production of high-quality, safely built housing, the coalition will consider the responsibility of the applicant to the community, as evidenced by the applicant's history of compliance with all local, state, and federal laws.

Housing Action Coalition Support

HAC support may include any or all of the following:

⊙ A letter of support for the project from the Housing Action Coalition that can be publicly circulated at the discretion of the developer;

⊙ Support letters from individual HAC members and organizations can be written for public circulation;

⊙ Active advocacy of the project, including testimony at public hearings by a HAC representative; and

⊙ HAC and organizational advocacy of the project, including public hearing testimony by a HAC representative, as well as by HAC members representing their individual organizations.

Tips on Working Successfully with the Media

The media can be a powerful tool in advancing your smart growth agenda. Learning to work with members of the media requires a common sense approach. Reviewing the following tips will help you to be better prepared to capitalize on the public relations opportunities that a good relationship with your local media can provide.

Establish a good relationship with the media. Media representatives are human beings just like other professionals. They have specific strengths and weaknesses, likes and dislikes. It takes time, work, patience, and tolerance to develop mutual trust and respect. You should initiate meetings with members of the media.

Make yourself a preferred source. As media representatives get to know you personally, they will be more willing to listen to your "news." And if they listen, your programs and initiatives will be more likely to receive positive coverage. Familiarizing yourself with the media and understanding the publication you are pitching will give the writer more confidence in you as a reliable source of information.

Be aware of your common audience. You and the media share the same audience—the public. Media representatives have an obligation to provide information to the public and you can play a role in helping to keep the public informed.

Call the media at convenient times. Daily newspaper reporters are typically on deadline from 3:00 p.m. on; it is best not to call them then. Television reporters edit their pieces to make the evening news. They, too, are hard to reach in the afternoon. Radio personalities, obviously, are unavailable when they are on the air. They typically can be reached for several hours after airtime.

Know the appropriate person to contact.

Television stations. After faxing a press release or media advisory to your local station, follow up with a call. Ask for the assignment editor and ask him or her if he or she has any questions about the event.

Daily newspapers. You most likely will send your information to the local news editor at your local paper. Other possibilities include the real estate or lifestyle editors.

Weekly newspapers. Community newspapers also can be a good outlet. If you are holding a community outreach event, submit a brief press release with the essential information: who, what, when, where, and a contact name and number.

Prepare for bad news. The secret to managing bad news is to take action in the first few minutes or hours of a crisis. Do not hesitate. When something has gone wrong and it is your fault, send in the right spokesperson early. If necessary, have experts available to explain what happened and how it will be addressed.

Source: *52 Common Sense Tips on Working with the Media* (Walnut Creek, California: Gallen Associates, Inc., 2000).

Smart Growth Contacts

Organization/Agency/Community	World Wide Web Address	Phone Number
American Farmland Trust	www.farmland.org	202-331-7300
American Institute of Architects–Center for Livable Communities	www.e-architect.com	202-626-7406
American Planning Association	www.planning.org	312-431-9100
Bank of America–Environmental Programs	www.bankamerica.com/environment	650-615-4700
Center for Livable Communities	www.lgc.org/clc	800-290-8202
Center for Neighborhood Technology	www.cnt.org	773-278-4800
Congress for the New Urbanism	www.cnu.org	415-495-2255
The Conservation Fund	www.conservationfund.org	703-525-6300
Georgia Regional Transportation Authority	www.grta.org	404-463-6000
International City/County Management Association	www.icma.org	202-289-4262
Local Government Commission	www.lgc.org	916-448-1198
National Association of Counties	www.naco.org	202-393-6226
National Association of Home Builders	www.nahb.com	800-368-5242
National Association of Local Government Environmental Professionals	www.nalgep.org	202-638-6254
National Association of Realtors	nar.realtor.com	202-383-1014
National League of Cities	www.nlc.org	202-626-3000
National Trust for Historic Preservation	www.nthp.org	202-588-6000
Smart Growth Network	www.smartgrowth.org	202-260-2750
State of Maryland Smart Growth and Neighborhood Conservation	www.mdp.state.md.us	410-767-4500
Surface Transportation Policy Project	www.transact.org	202-466-2636
The Trust for Public Land	www.tpl.org	415-495-4014
ULI–the Urban Land Institute	www.uli.org	202-624-7000
U.S. Conference of Mayors and National Association of Counties Joint Center for Sustainable Communities	www.usmayors.org/USCM/sustainable	202-861-6773 or 202-942-4224
U.S. Environmental Protection Agency	www.epa.gov	202-260-4048

ULI Smart Growth Resources

Smart Growth News. Prepared for members of ULI–the Urban Land Institute and others, *Smart Growth News* provides biweekly e-mail briefings on smart growth policies and development practices gathered from a media sweep of more than 1,400 information sources, including major national newspapers, business magazines, other periodicals, Web sites, and national and international wire services. To subscribe, go to www.uli.org and click on "E-News," then on "Smart Growth."

Community outreach initiative. This ULI program is designed to provide communities with strategic technical assistance, best practice examples, and financial resources to advance and lend value to locally driven smart growth programs. The community outreach initiative is largely supported by the Bank of America, the Irvine Foundation, and the ULI Foundation.

Books. ULI has published numerous books on a wide variety of smart growth–related issues, including the following:

Density by Design: New Directions in Residential Development;

Developing Urban Entertainment Centers;

The Dimensions of Parking;

Implementing Smart Growth at the Local Level;

Inside City Parks;

Moving Beyond Gridlock: Traffic and Development;

Multifamily Housing Development Handbook;

The Practice of Sustainable Development;

Smart Growth: Myth and Fact;

Trends and Innovations in Master-Planned Communities;

Turning Brownfields into Greenbacks: Developing and Financing Environmentally Contaminated Land; and

Valuing the New Urbanism.

Conferences and programs. ULI holds a variety of conferences and educational programs that address smart growth issues, including program sessions at its annual meetings and the following conferences. The **Partners for Smart Growth Conference,** the premier national conference on smart growth, features specific best-practice examples of smart growth projects and highlights the latest smart growth trends. The annual conference brings together public sector officials, developers, and civic and environmental interests to discuss the challenges and lessons learned in the advancement of smart growth. **Place Making: Developing Town Centers, Transit Villages, and Main Streets,** another annual conference, brings together leading land use practitioners, including developers, architects, financiers, consultants, and public officials, to explore techniques to create and enhance town centers, transit villages, and main streets in America's cities and suburbs.